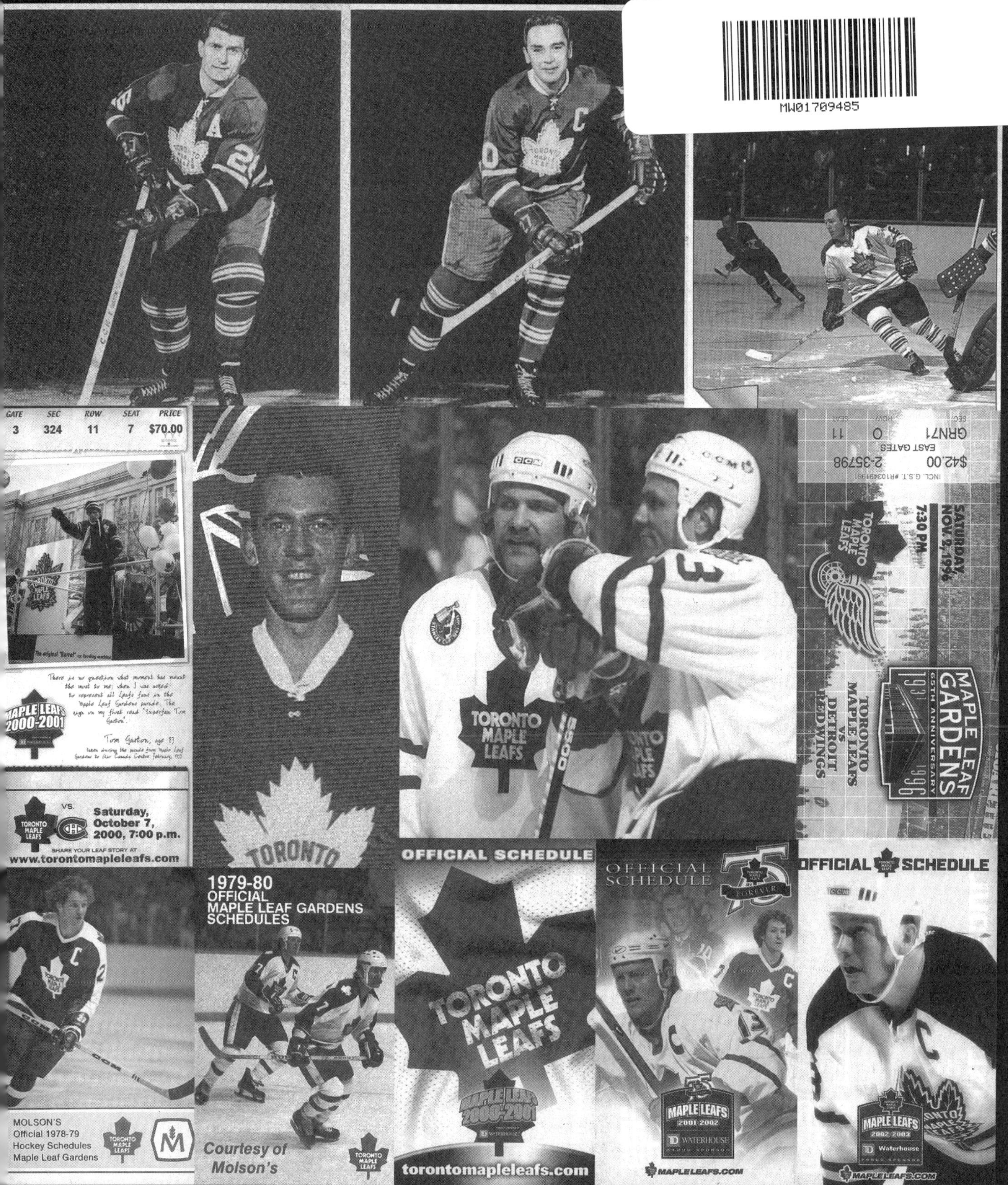
GATE SEC ROW SEAT PRICE
3 324 11 7 $70.00
The original "Barrel"
There is no question what moment has meant the most to me; when I was asked to represent all Leafs fans in the Maple Leaf Gardens parade. The sign on my float read "Superfan Tom Gaston".
Tom Gaston, age 83
MAPLE LEAFS 2000-2001
TORONTO MAPLE LEAFS
VS.
Saturday, October 7, 2000, 7:00 p.m.
SHARE YOUR LEAF STORY AT
www.torontomapleleafs.com
TORONTO
TORONTO MAPLE LEAFS
SATURDAY NOV. 2, 1996
7:30 PM
$42.00
EAST GATES
GRN71
MAPLE LEAF GARDENS
65TH ANNIVERSARY
1931 1996
TORONTO MAPLE LEAFS VS DETROIT REDWINGS
MOLSON'S
Official 1978-79
Hockey Schedules
Maple Leaf Gardens
1979-80
OFFICIAL
MAPLE LEAF GARDENS
SCHEDULES
Courtesy of Molson's
OFFICIAL SCHEDULE
TORONTO MAPLE LEAFS
MAPLE LEAFS 2000-2001
torontomapleleafs.com
OFFICIAL SCHEDULE
FOREVER
MAPLE LEAFS 2001 2002
TD WATERHOUSE
MAPLELEAFS.COM
OFFICIAL SCHEDULE
MAPLE LEAFS 2002 2003
TD Waterhouse
MAPLELEAFS.COM

The Maple Leafs Trivia Book 1927–2003

TORONTO
MAPLE
LEAFS

Mike Leonetti

The Maple Leafs Trivia Book

1927–2003

HarperCollinsPublishersLtd

The Maple Leafs Trivia Book, 1927–2003

First published in paperback by HarperCollins Publishers Ltd. 2000. Revised and expanded paperback edition 2003.

HarperCollins books may be purchased for educational, business, or sales promotional use through our Special Markets Department.

HarperCollins Publishers Ltd.
2 Bloor Street East, 20th Floor
Toronto, Ontario, Canada
M4W 1A8

www.harpercanada.com

National Library of Canada Cataloguing in Publication

Leonetti, Mike, 1958–
The Maple Leafs trivia book, 1927–2003 /
Mike Leonetti. – Rev. and expanded.

Previous ed. published under title:
The illustrated Toronto Maple Leafs trivia book.
ISBN 0-00-639457-4

1. Toronto Maple Leafs (Hockey team) – Miscellanea.
I. Title.

GV848.T6L46 2003 796.962'64'09713541 C2003-903770-3

TC 9 8 7 6 5 4 3 2

Printed and bound in Canada
Set in Minion and Eras

The fourth edition of The Maple Leafs Trivia Book *is dedicated to the 25 players named as the greatest Leafs of all time and to four of them in particular:*
Johnny Bower, Dave Keon,
Frank Mahovlich and
Darryl Sittler.

DAVE KEON

FRANK MAHOVLICH

DARRYL SITTLER

Contents

Acknowledgements

The author would like to thank the following people for their assistance:
Allan Anshan, Harold Barkley, Hartwell Bowsfied, Chris Bucci, Craig Campbell, Dan Diamond, Jack Felstead, Gino Granieri, Bill Gray, William Houston, Jim Hughson, Kim Lennox, Don Loney, John Maiola, Dennis Miles, Paul Patzkou, Andrew Podnieks, Joseph Romain, Michael Sabadash, Gord Stellick and James Williamson. Many thanks to Susan Young for her help and dedication to this project. A special thank you to Maria and David Leonetti for their support and understanding.

Photographs provided by:

Harold Barkley Archives
Graphic Artists, Hockey Hall of Fame
Lou and Nat Turofsky, Hockey Hall of Fame
John Maiola
Dennis Miles
Robert Shaver
St. Lawrence Starch Company
Toronto Maple Leafs
Toronto Star
Jim Wiley
York University Archives

Introduction

The Toronto Maple Leafs last won the Stanley Cup in 1967 when I was eight years old and the country of Canada was celebrating its 100th birthday. It was the best of times as the Leafs beat the Montreal Canadiens in six great games to win their 11th Cup. I remember keeping a scrapbook at the time marking the occasion of the Centennial and of a somewhat unexpected triumph for my favourite hockey team. I cut out every hockey picture I could get my hands on from the local newspapers as the Leafs first eliminated Chicago (who had finished first) and then beat the mighty Habs. To top it all off, my hero, Dave Keon, won the Conn Smythe Trophy as the best player in the

Leafs captain George Armstrong accepts the 1967 Stanley Cup.

playoffs! I no longer have the scrapbook (I lost it sometime after I left Grade 2) but I have never lost the memories or the great feeling of watching my team win the most prized trophy in all of sports.

The Maple Leafs Trivia Book 1927–2003, fourth edition, was written especially for fans like myself who remember the great moments and who would love nothing more than to see the blue and white return to their former glory. Leafs fans are special. Young or old, they are the most loyal in all of professional sports and should be commended for giving the Leafs organization the support it needs to build a winning team. It has been 36 years since the Maple Leafs carried the Stanley Cup off the ice, but perhaps one day in the not-too-distant future, Toronto management will do enough to bring the city a championship. In the meantime, we have many great moments and some terrific heroes to remember. There is no better way to do this than with some interesting trivia questions and exciting photos that highlight the long and storied history of this hockey team.

In all, this book contains about 600 questions and answers covering the years 1927 to 2003. You will find that there is an emphasis on the years from 1960 to 2003. This was done so that younger Leafs fans will be able to enjoy this book. The information in this book was put together from Leafs media guides, game programs, books, newspaper and magazine articles, radio and television broadcasts and other reliable sources. Every attempt has been made to ensure that all information is accurate. Any errors are those of the author.

It's still every child's dream to put on a Leafs sweater and play for the team that plays on *Hockey Night in Canada*. For the chosen few who have realized that dream, life has changed forever. For those of us who couldn't make it to the NHL, there are the moments and memories that go with being a fan. Leafs history is filled with heroes and legends that will always be part of a great city and indeed part of a great country. Leafs fans can be found all over Canada, and the blue and white sweaters come out whenever the team visits Montreal, Ottawa, Calgary, Edmonton or Vancouver. No other team in Canada (perhaps no other team in all of the NHL) enjoys such support, and now the team has its very own television station—Leafs TV. How many other teams can say that?

I sincerely hope you find this an enjoyable book and that you will be able to use it as a reference guide when you remember the great moments in Leafs history!

MIKE LEONETTI
July 1, 2003
Toronto, Ontario

The Maple Leafs Trivia Book 1927–2003

1

Memorable Games

1) The first game ever played at Maple Leaf Gardens took place on November 12, 1931, when Toronto faced the Chicago Blackhawks. Who scored the first goal at the Gardens? Who scored the first Leafs goal? What was the final score of the game?

2) The Toronto Maple Leafs won their first Stanley Cup in 1931–32—the first season they played at Maple Leaf Gardens. The final game of the best-of-five series (won by the Leafs in three straight) was played at the Gardens. Who scored the Leafs' first Stanley Cup–winning goal and what team did the Leafs defeat?

3) On April 13, 1933, the Leafs played in their longest overtime game in team history. Played at Maple Leaf Gardens against the Boston Bruins, the fifth and deciding game of the semi-final series went into a sixth overtime period. The Leafs finally scored at 104:26 of overtime to win the game 1–0. Who scored the winning goal?

The first Stanley Cup-winning Leafs team of 1931–32

4) The Maple Leafs played in an unusual game on February 20, 1944. Not only did the game end up 0–0, but it was also penalty free—the only time this has happened in an NHL game. Where did the game take place and who was the opponent?

Ted Kennedy and the Stanley Cup

5) In the 1942 Stanley Cup finals, the Maple Leafs staged the greatest comeback in hockey history. After losing the first three games, the Leafs came back to tie the series with 4–3, 9–3 and 3–0 victories. The seventh game was played on April 18, 1942, at Maple Leaf Gardens, with the Leafs winning 3–1 to capture the Stanley Cup. Which player scored the winning goal to complete this dramatic comeback?

6) In the 1945 Stanley Cup finals, the Leafs jumped out to a three-game-to-nothing advantage by beating Detroit 1–0, 2–0 and 1–0. However, the Red Wings won the next three games to tie the series and force a seventh game at the Detroit Olympia on April 22, 1945. With the score tied 1–1, the Leafs scored late in the third period to win the game 2–1 and take the Stanley Cup back to Toronto. Who scored the winning goal?

7) The first game of the 1950 Stanley Cup semifinals between the Maple Leafs and Red Wings played in Detroit on March 28, 1950, was one of the most controversial ever played between these two great rivals. It was in this game that Gordie Howe crashed into the boards while attempting to check a Leafs player. Howe was seriously injured and came close to death. Although the facts showed otherwise, the Red Wings blamed the Leafs player whom Howe was trying to check. Who was the Maple Leaf involved?

The Stanley Cup-winning goal in 1951—the most memorable in Leafs history.

8) After winning the Stanley Cup in 1947, 1948 and 1949, the Leafs were trying for their fourth straight championship in 1950. The Leafs faced the Detroit Red Wings in the first round of the 1950 playoffs. In a long, hard-fought and controversial semi-final series, the Red Wings finally prevailed by winning the seventh game in overtime. Can you name the goal scorer who put an end to the Leafs' hopes for a fourth straight Cup?

Dick Duff (#9) played many great games in the playoffs.

9) On their way to winning the Stanley Cup in 1951, the Leafs faced the Montreal Canadiens in the finals. The Leafs won the series 4 games to 1 with each game going into overtime. The fifth and final game of the series was played in Toronto on April 21, 1951. The Stanley Cup–winning goal—perhaps the most memorable in Leaf history—was scored by a defenceman who, it turned out, was playing in his last game. Who scored the goal and why was this his last game?

10) The first official NHL All-Star Game was played on October 13, 1947, at Maple Leaf Gardens between the Stanley Cup champion Maple Leafs and the NHL All-Stars. Who won the game?

11) On March 16, 1957, the Leafs set a team record by scoring 14 goals in one game. The Leafs won the game 14–1. Where was the game played and who was the opponent?

12) In 1958–59, George "Punch" Imlach took control of the team behind the bench with the Leafs in last place. The Leafs passed Detroit but trailed the fourth-place New York Rangers by seven points with only five games to play. In a miracle finish, the Leafs made the playoffs on the final night of the season. New York lost 4–2 to Montreal, while the Leafs beat Detroit 6–4 at the Olympia. Who scored the winning goal for Toronto to break a 4–4 tie and get the Maple Leafs into the post-season?

13) In the 1959 Stanley Cup finals, the Leafs faced the Montreal Canadiens. The Habs won the series 4 games to 1. The only game the Leafs won was in overtime 3–2 at home. Who scored the winning goal?

14) The first time the Leafs appeared in the Stanley Cup finals during the 1960s was in 1960 when they lost in four games straight to Montreal. In order to reach the finals that

year, the Leafs defeated Detroit in the semi-finals 4 games to 2. The third game of the Toronto–Detroit series went into a third overtime period before the Leafs finally scored to clinch a 5–4 victory. Can you name the player who scored the winning goal?

Dave Keon (#14) always scored important goals against the Montreal Canadiens.

15) The third game of the 1960 Stanley Cup finals between Montreal and Toronto was played on April 12, 1960, at the Gardens. In that game, Montreal's Maurice "Rocket" Richard scored his last NHL goal. Montreal won the game 5–2 and the series in four straight. Which Leafs goalie allowed the Rocket's final NHL goal?

Eddie Shack carries off the 1963 Stanley Cup.

16) On their way to the 1961–62 Stanley Cup, the Leafs played the New York Rangers in the semi-finals. It took Toronto six games to win the series, with the key game being the fifth. The series was tied at two games each when the crucial fifth game went into double overtime before the Leafs finally scored the winner. Can you name the player who scored the winner?
Hint: He later went on to coach the Maple Leafs.

17) The 1962 Stanley Cup final series between Toronto and Chicago was deadlocked at two games each, making the fifth game in Toronto crucial. However, it turned out to be a one-sided game when the Leafs won 8–4. Two nights later the Leafs won the series in the Chicago Stadium. In that 8–4 victory, the Leafs were led by one player who scored a hat trick to key the Leafs attack. Can you name the player who scored these important goals?

18) The Leafs' first Stanley Cup of the 1960s was won on the road in Chicago in April 1962. The Leafs won the finals in six games. In game six, Bobby Hull opened the scoring but Bob Nevin tied it for Toronto. Can you name the player who scored the winning goal, enabling the Leafs to win the game 2–1 and capture their first Stanley Cup in 11 years?
Hint: This player went on to become an assistant coach with Toronto in the 1979–80 season.

NHL president Clarence Campbell presents the 1963 Stanley Cup to the Leafs.

19) The last Maple Leafs team to finish in first place in the six-team league was the 1962–63 squad. That team also went on to capture the Stanley Cup. The game that clinched first place was played on March 20, 1963, at the Gardens, when the Leafs finished in a 3–3 tie against the Montreal Canadiens on a goal scored with eight seconds to play. Can you name the player who scored the first-place clincher?
Hint: The player who scored the goal would play many years later on a Leafs team with the goaltender he beat. In fact, both would make the NHL second All-Star team as members of the Leafs for the 1970–71 season.

Andy Bathgate holds up the 1964 Stanley Cup.

The Maple Leafs gather around the 1964 Stanley Cup.

20) In the fifth game of the 1962–63 finals between the Leafs and the Detroit Red Wings, Toronto scored a 3–1 victory to clinch the Stanley Cup. Two of the Leafs' goals were shorthanded efforts by one player, marking the first time this was done in an NHL playoff game. Can you name the player who scored the goals?
Hint: He is tied for the team record for most shorthanded goals in one season (eight), a mark he established in 1970–71.

21) On April 18, 1963, the Leafs defeated the Detroit Red Wings 3–1, thus winning the Stanley Cup on home ice for the first time since 1951. Can you name the player who scored the winning goal when the Leafs won the series 4 games to 1?

22) During the 1964 semi-finals, the Leafs played the Montreal Canadiens in a series that went the full seven games. The last game was played in Montreal. Backed by the superlative goaltending of Johnny Bower, the Leafs won 3–1. All the Toronto goals were scored by the same player. Can you name him?

23) In the first game of the 1964 Stanley Cup finals versus Detroit, Toronto won the game 3–2 on a goal scored with just two seconds left to play while the Leafs were shorthanded on home ice. Can you name the player who scored this dramatic goal that helped Toronto get off to a good start in the series?

George Armstrong skates off with the 1967 Stanley Cup.

24) The 1964 Stanley Cup finals between the Leafs and Red Wings marked the first time in five years that a game in the finals went into overtime. The second game of the series at Maple Leaf Gardens was won by Detroit 3–2. Who scored the winner in overtime?
Hint: He later played for Toronto.

25) During the sixth game of the 1964 Stanley Cup finals, a Leafs defenceman provided one of the greatest moments in playoff history. After being carted off the ice on a stretcher, he came back in the overtime period to score the winning goal, allowing the Leafs to win the game 4–3. That win sent the series back to Toronto for a seventh game, which the Leafs won to capture their third consecutive Stanley Cup. After the series was over, it was revealed that the defenceman had played the sixth and seventh games with a broken leg. Can you name this courageous player?

26) The 1964 Stanley Cup finals went to the seventh game at Maple Leaf Gardens. It was on April 25, 1964, when the Leafs shut out the Detroit Red Wings 4–0 to win their third straight championship. It also marked the second straight year the Leafs won the Cup on home ice. The winning goal came quickly at 3:04 of the first period. Can you name the player who scored the winning goal?
Hint: This player went on to play for the Red Wings and later for Pittsburgh, and was a former Hart Trophy winner.

27) The Leafs' reign of three consecutive championships (1962, 1963, 1964) was put to an end by the Montreal Canadiens in the 1965 semi finals. The series went six games: Montreal won it at the Gardens with an overtime goal. Can you name the Montreal player who scored the goal to end the Leafs' hopes for a fourth straight Stanley Cup?

28) In the 1967 Stanley Cup finals between Toronto and Montreal, the crucial third game went into double overtime at Maple Leaf Gardens. The Leafs finally scored to take the lead in the series 2 games to 1, and eventually went on to capture the Stanley Cup. Can

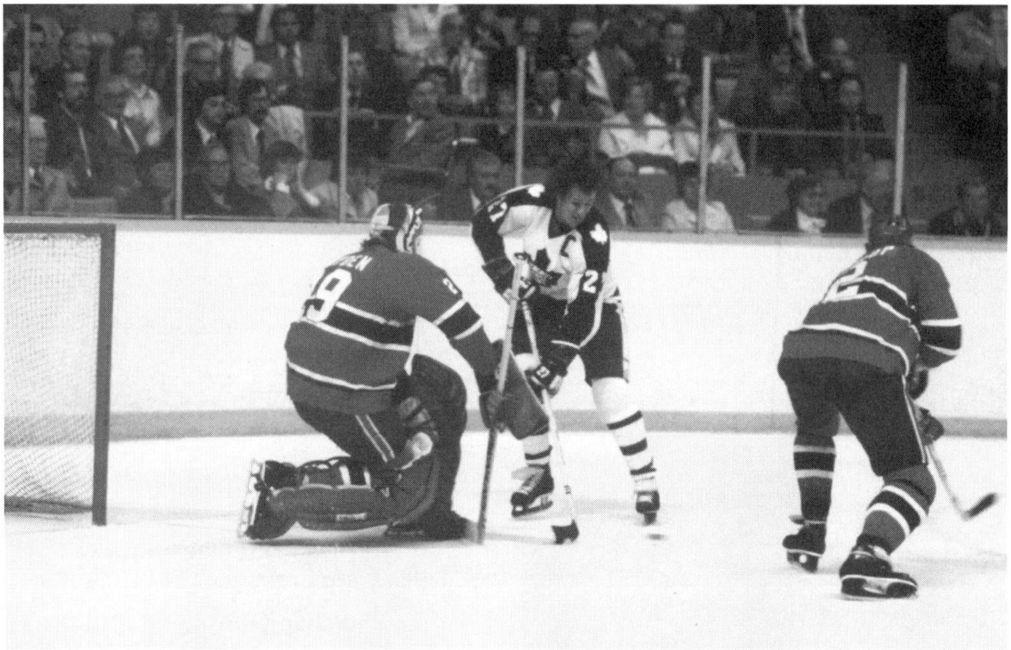

Darryl Sittler (#27) looks for the puck against Ken Dryden of the Montreal Canadiens.

you name the player who scored this key goal?
Hint: The player who scored the winner would later coach the goaltender he beat.

29) In the sixth and what turned out to be the last game of the 1967 Stanley Cup finals between Toronto and Montreal, the Leafs were protecting a 2–1 lead with a face-off in their own end with a little over a minute left in the game. Punch Imlach sent out his old veterans to preserve the victory. The Leafs not only stopped the Canadiens, but also scored a goal into the empty net. Can you name the player who scored the insurance goal to clinch the victory for this final Stanley Cup of the 1960s?
Hint: He later went on to coach the Toronto Marlboros to two Memorial Cups.

30) In their 1969 quarter-final playoff series, the Boston Bruins beat the Maple Leafs 10–0 and 7–0 in the first two games. They swept the series with two more wins in Toronto. What happened immediately after the final game on April 6, 1969?

31) On January 2, 1971, at Maple Leaf Gardens, the Leafs inflicted the worst defeat ever on an old rival from the six-team league. Who was the opponent and what was the score?

32) In the 1971 quarter-final series between the Leafs and the New York Rangers, the second game at Madison Square Garden featured a great deal of brawling, with Toronto winning the contest 4–1. During the fighting, an unusual incident took place. One of the Ranger forwards threw the face mask of the Leafs goaltender into the crowd and, naturally,

the New York fans did not return it, forcing the Leafs to use their backup goaltender. Who threw the mask into the crowd and who was the Leafs' starting goalie that night?

33) In the 1971 Stanley Cup playoffs, the Leafs were eliminated by the New York Rangers in a six-game quarter-final series. In the last game of the series, the Leafs scored a late goal to send it into overtime. However, the Rangers scored to win the game 2–1 and take the series. Can you name the player who scored the winner, and the Leafs goaltender?
Hint: The goal scorer was a former Leaf and the goaltender he beat was a former Ranger.

34) The 1972 playoffs ended quickly for the Leafs. They were knocked out in five games by the Boston Bruins, who went on to win the Stanley Cup. The only game the Leafs did win was a 4–3 overtime triumph at the Boston Garden. Can you name the player who beat Gerry Cheevers to provide the only Toronto highlight of the series?
Hint: He was a former Bruin who was traded to Toronto in exchange for Wayne Carlton. He also scored 10 points in one game while with Edmonton of the WHA in January 1973.

35) The Leafs did not have much luck with playoff games that went into overtime at Maple Leaf Gardens during the 1970s. In fact, the last time the Leafs won an overtime game at home during the '70s was on April 10, 1975, when Toronto defeated the Los Angeles Kings 3–2 during the preliminary round (best-of-three) playoff series. Can you name the player who scored the winning goal?

Lanny McDonald gathers in the puck against the Minnesota North Stars.

36) Darryl Sittler had a spectacular night on February 7, 1976, against the Boston Bruins in an 11–4 victory at Maple Leaf Gardens. He scored 10 points on six goals and four assists, setting a new NHL record for most points in one game. Can you name the goaltender who was playing in the net for the Bruins that night, and the Leaf who got the goal Sittler did not pick up a scoring point on?

37) Darryl Sittler had a record performance on April 22, 1976, against the Philadelphia Flyers in the playoffs. In that game, won by Toronto 8–5, Sittler scored five goals to tie the NHL record for most goals in one playoff game. Can you name the Philadelphia goaltender on that evening?
Hint: The goaltender was a former teammate of Sittler's.

Eddie Olczyk

Ian Turnbull (#2) had a big night against the Detroit Red Wings in 1977.

38) During a bitter and controversial seven-game quarter-final series between Toronto and Philadelphia in April 1976, three Flyers were charged with criminal offences after the third game. It was a very hot evening in Toronto, and the fighting seemed to be more important than the hockey. Can you name the Philadelphia players who were charged by Toronto police?

Glenn Anderson

39) Darryl Sittler's dramatic overtime goal in the 1976 Canada Cup defeated Czechoslovakia 5–4, clinching the Canada Cup for Team Canada. Can you name the goaltender Sittler beat?

40) In April 1977, the Leafs played the Pittsburgh Penguins in the best-of-three preliminary round playoff series. The series went the full three games and the Leafs won the third game on the strength of a hat trick by a Leafs winger. Can you name the Leaf who scored three goals to clinch the series for Toronto?

41) On February 2, 1977, the Leafs' Ian Turnbull became the first defenceman in NHL history to score five goals in one game in a 9–1 rout of the Detroit Red Wings. Turnbull did it in only five shots, all in the second and third periods. He beat two Detroit goaltenders. Can you name both of them?

42) During the 1977 quarter-final series with the Philadelphia Flyers, the Leafs won the first two games in the Spectrum. However, they lost the next two games at the Gardens—both heartbreaking overtime losses. The Leafs eventually lost the series in six games. In the fourth game, the Leafs had a 5–2 lead turn into a 6–5 overtime loss—spoiling the four-goal performance by one Leaf. Can you name the Leafs player who turned in a great performance in a losing cause?

Wendel Clark had a great playoff round in 1993.

43) Although the Russians toured North America many times during the mid- and late 1970s, the Leafs never played against them as a team. However, in January 1978 the Leafs did play the Kladno team from Czechoslovakia at Maple Leaf Gardens. Do you remember the result of the Leafs' first international clash and why controversy surrounded the game?

Opening night at the Air Canada Centre with Vince Damphousse and Mats Sundin taking the ceremonial face-off.

44) The Leafs won their 1978 quarter-final series against the New York Islanders in a hard-fought seven-game series. However, the situation did not appear to be especially bright after the fourth game when All-Star defenceman Borje Salming accidentally received an Islander stick in the eye, knocking him out of that series and the rest of the playoffs with a serious injury. Can you name the Islanders player involved in the incident?

45) In 1978 the Maple Leafs defeated the New York Islanders in a very physical series that went the full seven games. The Leafs won the seventh game in New York on an overtime goal. Can you name the player who scored the goal to send the Leafs to the semi-finals—their best showing since their 1967 Stanley Cup win?

46) Most Leafs fans remember Darryl Sittler's 10-point night against Boston in 1976. However, Sittler had another big night at Maple Leaf Gardens during the home opener for the 1978–79 season on October 14, 1978. In that game, Sittler scored three goals and added four assists for a total of seven points when Toronto won the game 10–7. Can you name the team the Leafs were playing that night and the opposing goaltender(s)?

47) One of the most memorable games played at Maple Leaf Gardens during the 1970s was the third game of the 1979 quarter-final playoff series against Montreal. It was a game the Leafs had to win, but in the second overtime period a little-used opposition player scored the winner, giving Montreal a 4–3 win and a three-game lead in the series, which they went on to win in four straight. Can you name the player who scored the winner? *Hint: He went on to play for the New York Rangers and the Edmonton Oilers.*

48) The last game of the 1979 quarter-final series between Toronto and Montreal is one Leafs fans are likely to remember. After trailing 4–0 in the game, the Leafs roared back to tie 4–4. The game went into overtime. However, the overtime period ended in controversy when the Leafs were assessed a questionable penalty, with Montreal scoring on the subsequent power play. Can you name the player who received the penalty and the player who scored, allowing Montreal to win the game 5–4 and sweep the series 4 games to 0?

49) On March 19, 1981, the Leafs suffered one of their worst defeats ever. In fact, they allowed a club record: most goals ever by one team in a single game—14. They lost the game 4–14. Where was the game played and who was the opposition?

50) On January 8, 1986, the Leafs were involved in the highest-scoring game in team history. The goal total for both teams combined reached 20—just one short of the NHL record. What was the final score and who was the opposition?

51) In the 1986 playoffs, the Leafs defeated the Chicago Blackhawks in three straight games and took the St. Louis Blues to a seventh game. One player led the team with three game-winning goals in the playoffs. His first was in Chicago as the Leafs rallied to win the second game of their series with the Blackhawks 6–4. His second game winner came in the Leafs' third and last match against the Hawks—a 7–2 romp. His final game winner snapped a 3–3 third-period tie at the Gardens between the Leafs and Blues, forcing a seventh and deciding game. Which player scored these dramatic goals?

52) On April 9, 1987, the Leafs won their first overtime playoff game on the road since 1978, when they defeated the St. Louis Blues 3–2 in the fifth game of the Norris Division semi-finals. The winning goal was fired in by a defenceman. Can you name the goal scorer?

53) In the 1987 playoffs, the Leafs won a best-of-seven playoff series for the first time since 1978, by upsetting the St. Louis Blues in six games. The sixth game, played at Maple Leaf Gardens, was won by Toronto 4–0. In addition to the stellar goaltending of Ken Wregget, the Leafs were led by the player who scored the winning goal in the final game. This player was better known as "Motor City." Can you name him?

54) The Leafs won their first overtime playoff game since 1975 when they defeated Detroit 3–2 in the fourth game of the 1987 Norris Division finals. The player who scored the winning goal had been acquired in a deal with the New York Rangers in which the Leafs gave up Walt Poddubny. Can you name him?

55) After a poor season in 1987–88 (only 52 points), the Leafs met the Detroit Red Wings in the Norris Division semi-finals. In the fourth game of the series, the Red Wings humiliated the Leafs 8–0. The fans added to the embarrassment by pelting the Gardens ice with everything possible, including Leafs sweaters and souvenir pucks. In spite of this, the Leafs went to Detroit and won the fifth game 6–5, largely because of a hat trick scored by one player that included the game winner just 34 seconds into overtime. It marked the first time since 1978 that a Leafs player scored three goals in a playoff game.

Although the Leafs lost the series, this performance certainly helped to restore some pride within the Leafs organization after one of its worst defeats. Can you name the player who netted the three goals?

56) During the 1990 playoffs, the Leafs faced the St. Louis Blues and were defeated in five games. They lost the third game at Maple Leaf Gardens when the Blues scored in overtime to give them a 3–0 lead in the series. Who scored the Blues marker and who was in net for the Leafs?
Hint: The St. Louis goal scorer would go on to play for the Leafs.

Nikolai Borschevsky

57) A small player with good hands and a goal-scoring touch, this Russian-born left winger scored the goal that eliminated the Detroit Red Wings during a memorable seven-game series in the 1993 playoffs. Name him.

58) In the second round of the 1993 playoffs, the Leafs met the St. Louis Blues in a series that would go seven games. The Leafs got off to a good start by beating the Blues in double overtime in the first game, but lost the second contest, also in double overtime, when a Blues defenceman jumped into the play and scored the winner. Who scored the Leafs' winner (against Curtis Joseph) and who got the Blues' marker (versus Felix Potvin)?

59) When the Leafs won the fifth game of the Campbell Conference finals in 1993 against the Los Angeles Kings, it looked like they were headed to the finals (and a meeting with the Montreal Canadiens!) The Leafs won the fifth game at the Gardens on a clutch goal by which Toronto winger?
Hint: This player is second all-time for the most overtime winning goals in NHL playoff history (five).

60) Wendel Clark's greatest game as a Leaf was the sixth game of the 1993 playoff series against Los Angeles. Clark scored three times (the final goal came late in regulation time to tie the score 4–4), but an overtime goal by Wayne Gretzky ended the game on a Kings power play. Gretzky should have been in the penalty box for cutting the Leafs' Doug Gilmour with his stick. Which referee choked on the obvious call and allowed Gretzky to stay on the ice?

Garry Valk

61) Wayne Gretzky scored three goals during a 5–4 win over the Leafs on May 29, 1993, to send his Los Angeles Kings to the Stanley Cup finals. Gretzky's last goal turned out to be the eventual game winner, but the most crucial goal was scored when the game was tied 3–3 late in the third period of the seventh game. Who scored the go-ahead goal?

62) The San Jose Sharks surprised the Maple Leafs in the second round of the 1994 playoffs and forced the Toronto club to a seventh game. The Leafs were actually trailing the Sharks 3–2 in the series when they won the sixth game in overtime to force a deciding contest. Who scored the overtime winner? *Hint: This player was a late-season acquisition and also scored the series-clinching goal when the Leafs knocked out Chicago in the first round of the 1994 post-season.*

63) May 16, 1994, saw the Maple Leafs win the first game of the Campbell Conference finals with a 3–2 overtime win at the Gardens. Four games later, on May 24, the Leafs were eliminated by the Vancouver Canucks in a 4–3 overtime loss. Who scored the Leafs' winner and which Canuck sent his team into the finals?

64) The last game played by the Leafs at Maple Leaf Gardens took place on February 13, 1999. It was a 6–2 loss to which team?

65) The first game played at the Air Canada Centre took place on February 20, 1999, against the Montreal Canadiens. The Leafs won the game 3–2 in overtime. Who scored the first Leafs goal and who scored the overtime winner?

66) In knocking out the Philadelphia Flyers in six games during the 1999 playoffs, the Leafs won the fifth game of the series at home on an overtime winner scored by a player the Leafs had re-acquired in a deal at the trade deadline. Name him.
Hint: The Leafs had originally selected this player in the third round of the 1991 entry draft.

67) After losing every previous playoff series against the Flyers, the Maple Leafs finally got some revenge against Philadelphia with their playoff win in 1999. The clinching game was played in Philadelphia, and this thrilling contest was decided by a Leafs power-play goal with just 59 seconds to play. Who scored the winner?

68) In defeating the Pittsburgh Penguins in six games during the second round of the 1999 playoffs, the Leafs won two of the contests in overtime. Name the two Leafs who scored the winning goals.

Toronto captain Mats Sundin

69) For the first time since 1968, the NHL All-Star Game returned to Toronto in February 2000 at the Air Canada Centre. Which three Maple Leafs from the 1999–2000 team played in the contest?

70) During the 1999–2000 season, the week of March 4–11 was very special for the Leafs because of something they accomplished right across Canada. What did the Leafs do that week?

71) The only highlight for Leafs fans in the 2000 playoffs was a first-round win over the Ottawa Senators. The fifth game was settled in overtime (2–1) and gave the Leafs the lead in this series, which they went on to win in six games. Who scored the crucial overtime winner?

72) In the first round of the 2001 playoffs, the Maple Leafs swept the Ottawa Senators. Their cause was greatly aided by two overtime winning goals, one in the first game and one in the third. The first OT winner came in Ottawa (securing a 1–0 win) by a very expected source of goal scoring, but the second marker (netting the Leafs a 3–2 victory at the ACC) was scored by a blueliner who was not a likely candidate to score such an important goal. Name the two goal getters.

73) Toronto lost the Eastern Conference semi-finals to New Jersey for a second straight year in 2001 when they lost a seven-game series. Two of the losses that crushed the Leafs' hopes came in overtime in the second and third games. Who scored the winners for the Devils during those two contests?

74) The Maple Leafs bested the New York Islanders in the first round of the 2002 playoffs in a hard-fought seven-game series. The Leafs won the first two at home but lost the next two on Long Island. The fourth game of the series ended in controversial fashion as the Islanders were awarded a penalty shot that won them the game 4–3. Which Islander shooter beat Leafs goalie Curtis Joseph?

75) Toronto beat the Ottawa Senators in the playoffs for the third straight year during a seven-game series in 2002. The Leafs' second-

round win was highlighted by a 3–2 triple overtime win in the third contest played at the ACC. It was the fourth-longest game in Leafs history. Who scored the winner?

Gary Roberts signed with the Leafs as a free agent.

76) The Maple Leafs lost three overtime games (two of them on home ice) to the Carolina Hurricanes during the 2003 Eastern Conference finals. The losses ensured that the Leafs missed out on one of their best chances to advance to the Stanley Cup finals since 1967. Can you name the three members of the Hurricanes who scored the important overtime winners?

77) For the first time in 10 years the Maple Leafs had a player score three goals in one playoff game during the first round of the 2003 post-season, in the series against the Philadelphia Flyers. Who scored the hat trick on the road in the first game of the series?

78) Two of the Maple Leafs' victories over the Philadelphia Flyers in the 2003 Eastern Conference quarter-finals came in overtime at the ACC. Which two Leafs scored the winning goals in the second (a 4–3 win) and sixth (2–1) games?

79) Toronto and Philadelphia played the third-longest game in Maple Leafs history during the fourth game of the 2003 Eastern Conference quarter-finals at the ACC. Leafs goalie Ed Belfour made a team-record-setting 72 saves (out of 75 shots) in the contest that did not end until the third overtime period. A Leafs victory would have given Toronto a 3–1 series lead, but they went on to lose in seven games. Who scored the very important goal that won the contest 3–2 for the Flyers?

RED KELLY

Answers

1) Harold "Mush" March of Chicago scored the first goal. Charlie Conacher scored the first Leafs goal. Chicago won the game 2–1.
2) Ace Bailey scored the goal against the New York Rangers.
3) Ken Doraty
4) The game was played in the Chicago Stadium against the Blackhawks.
5) Pete Langelle
6) Walter "Babe" Pratt
7) Ted Kennedy
8) Leo Reise
9) Bill Barilko scored the goal, and was killed in a plane crash later in the summer of 1951.
10) All-Stars 4, Toronto 3
11) The game was played in Toronto against the New York Rangers.
12) Dick Duff

BOB BAUN

Alex Mogilny came to the Leafs as a free agent.

13) Dick Duff
14) Frank Mahovlich
15) Johnny Bower
16) Red Kelly scored the winner, putting the puck past Gump Worsley.
17) Bob Pulford
18) Dick Duff
19) Dave Keon scored on Canadiens goalie Jacques Plante.
20) Dave Keon
21) Eddie Shack
22) Dave Keon
23) Bob Pulford
24) Larry Jeffery
25) Bobby Baun
26) Andy Bathgate
27) Claude Provost
28) Bob Pulford scored the winner, beating Rogie Vachon.
29) George Armstrong
30) Leafs president Stafford Smythe fired long-time coach Punch Imlach.
31) The Leafs defeated the Detroit Red Wings 13–0.
32) Ranger Vic Hadfield threw Bernie Parent's mask into the stands, forcing Jacques Plante to take over.
33) Bob Nevin scored for the Rangers against the Leafs' Jacques Plante.
34) Jim Harrison
35) Blaine Stoughton
36) Dave Reece was the Boston goalie. George Ferguson scored the other Leafs goal.
37) Bernie Parent
38) Joe Watson, Mel Bridgman and Don Saleski
39) Vladimir Dzurilla
40) Lanny McDonald

Frank Mahovlich

The Leafs bench as the last game of the 1967 finals comes to an end.

Travis Green is proving to be a good playoff performer.

Goalie Ed Belfour has had an illustrious NHL career.

41) Three goals went past Eddie Giacomin and two went past Jim Rutherford.
42) Lanny McDonald
43) The Leafs lost to the Czech team 8–5. The controversy centred around the fact that the Leafs did not dress many of their regular players, including Borje Salming, Ian Turnbull, Lanny McDonald and Mike Palmateer.
44) Lorne Henning
45) Lanny McDonald
46) The opposition was the New York Islanders, with Billy Smith and Glenn Resch sharing the netminding.
47) Cam Connor
48) Dave "Tiger" Williams received the penalty and Larry Robinson was the goal scorer.
49) The game was played in the Buffalo Auditorium against the Sabres.
50) Toronto defeated the Edmonton Oilers 11–9.
51) Walt Poddubny
52) Rick Lanz
53) Brad Smith
54) Mike Allison
55) Eddie Olczyk
56) Sergio Momesso beat Allan Bester.
57) Nikolai Borschevsky
58) Doug Gilmour and Jeff Brown
59) Glenn Anderson
60) Kerry Fraser
61) Mike Donnelly
62) Mike Gartner
63) Peter Zezel and Greg Adams
64) The Chicago Blackhawks
65) Todd Warriner and Steve Thomas
66) Yanic Perreault
67) Sergei Berezin
68) Sergei Berezin in the fourth game and Garry Valk in the sixth game
69) Curtis Joseph, Mats Sundin and Dmitry Yushkevich
70) The Leafs defeated all the other Canadian teams—

Montreal 4–3, Vancouver 6–5 in overtime, Edmonton 2–0, Calgary 6–2 and Ottawa 4–2. The only game played at home was against the Canadiens.

71) Steve Thomas
72) Mats Sundin and Cory Cross
73) Randy McKay and Brian Rafalski
74) Shawn Bates
75) Gary Roberts
76) Niclas Wallin, Jeff O'Neill and Martin Gelinas
77) Alex Mogilny in a 5–3 win
78) Tomas Kaberle and Travis Green
79) Mark Recchi

The Maple Leafs acquired Mike Gartner (#11) in a late-season deal during 1993–94.

2

Records and Awards

1) Although no Maple Leaf has won the Art Ross Trophy (given to the leading point scorer for the regular schedule) since it was first awarded in 1948, Leafs players led the league in scoring in five seasons prior to 1948. Can you name the Leafs players who led the NHL in scoring prior to 1948?
Hint: There are only four players to be named, since one player did it twice.

2) Only three players have been on five Toronto Maple Leafs Stanley Cup–winning teams. Can you name them?

3) Five different Maple Leafs have led the NHL in goals scored during the regular season. One of these players did it four times and tied for the lead on another occasion. Can you name him and the four other players?

4) Which player holds the Leafs club record for being named to the NHL first All-Star Team most often? How many times was he named?

5) Prior to 1960, Maple Leafs goaltenders won the Vezina Trophy (then awarded for the fewest goals allowed in the regular season) on four occasions. Who were the goalies that won?
Hint: There is one double winner.

6) Prior to 1961, a Maple Leafs player was awarded the Lady Byng Trophy (given for sportsmanship combined with playing ability) on five occasions. Can you name the players who won the Lady Byng prior to 1961?
Hint: There is one double winner.

7) Between 1937 and 1961, seven Maple Leafs won the Calder Memorial Trophy, awarded to the rookie of the year. This includes a streak of three consecutive years between

Turk Broda and Ted Kennedy

1943 and 1945. Can you name all the winners?

8) Who coached the Leafs to the most Stanley Cup victories: Punch Imlach or Hap Day?

9) The last time a member of the Maple Leafs won the Hart Trophy (given to the most valuable player for the regular season) was back in 1955. In fact, only two Leafs have ever won this prestigious award. Can you name these two distinguished players?

10) Only two men have been in the general manager's chair when the Leafs won their 11 Stanley Cups. Who are they?

11) True or false? The Leafs share the league record for the fewest goals allowed in one season (at least a 70-game schedule) with the Montreal Canadiens.

12) The J.P. Bickell Memorial Trophy, first awarded in 1953, was given to honor a past president of Maple Leaf Gardens and was awarded to the most valuable Leafs player. Who won it the first time?

13) Which Leaf holds the team record for most goals scored in one period, and against what team did he set the mark?

14) The record fastest goal by a Leaf from the start of a game was scored seven seconds in. The record was set on February 6, 1932, in a 6–0 shutout of the Boston Bruins. Who scored the goal?

15) From 1926–27 to 1937–38, the NHL was divided into two divisions—a Canadian division and an American division. How many times did the Leafs finish first in the Canadian division?

16) In 1954–55 the Leafs set a team record for most ties in one season. How many ties did the team have during that 70-game season?

17) Who was the first Maple Leaf to score five goals in one game, and against what team?

Al Rollins

18) Only one Leafs centre has ever been chosen for the NHL first All-Star Team. He did it twice. Who was he?

19) After winning the Stanley Cup in 1951, the Maple Leafs went through some lean years between 1952 and 1959. This is evidenced by the fact that only two players made the NHL first All-Star Team during those seven years. Who were those two players?

20) How many games long is the Maple Leafs team record for longest winning streak from the start of the season?

21) Which two Leafs players hold the club record for the most assists in one game?

22) How many games long is the Maple Leafs team record for the longest undefeated streak?

23) Which Leafs goaltender holds the club record for most career shutouts, and how many?

24) During the 1962–63 season, a young Leafs defenceman, acquired from Springfield of the American Hockey League, won the Calder Trophy for being the best rookie that year. However, his career with the Leafs did not turn out to be a long one. In the expansion draft of 1967 he was taken by the Oakland Seals. He also played for Detroit. Can you name him?
Hint: This player was known for wearing charcoal under his eyes to help fight the glare of the bright television lights.

25) Only one Leaf has ever won the Conn Smythe Trophy as the outstanding player in the Stanley Cup playoffs. The year was 1967. Can you name the player?

26) The 1965–66 Calder Trophy winner was a Leafs winger who was taken from Toronto in the expansion draft of 1967 by Philadelphia. However, he would be re-acquired in a trade with the Flyers late in the 1968–69 season, only to be traded away to St. Louis early in 1970–71. Can you name this much-travelled former rookie of the year?

27) The 1960s featured Leafs teams that were known for their checking ability and solid defensive play, which helped them win the Vezina Trophy twice. Johnny Bower was the main puck-stopper during the 1960s and won the Vezina on his own for the 1960–61 season. The Leafs won their second Vezina of the decade for the 1964–65 season, but this time Bower shared it with another goalie. Can you name him?

28) The Lady Byng Trophy was won three consecutive times by Maple Leafs players, during the years 1961 to 1963. Can you name the Toronto recipients of the Lady Byng during those years?
Hint: There are only two players to be named since one player received the award twice.

29) Between 1970 and 1980, five members of the Maple Leafs were chosen as NHL All-Stars on either the first or the second team. One was a goaltender, one a defenceman and three were forwards. Can you name all five and name the player(s) who made the first team at least once?

Toronto's Sid Smith tries to score on Boston's Jim Henry.

30) Between 1960 and 1969, six Maple Leafs were selected as NHL All-Stars on either the first or the second team. One was a goaltender, three were defencemen and two were forwards. Can you name all six players and name those who made the first team at least once?

31) Can you name the first Leafs coach to be named the *Hockey News* coach of the year and the season in which he received this honor?
Hint: He later went on to become assistant general manager with the Leafs.

32) Terry Sawchuk's record of 103 career shutouts is not likely to be broken. While he was with the Leafs he recorded one very significant shutout on March 4, 1967, when the Leafs defeated Chicago 3–0. What was significant about that shutout?

33) Five players have played more than 1,000 games as members of the Maple Leafs. Can you name them?

34) From the 1959–60 season through to 1989–90, three Leafs led the league in penalty minutes for one year. Can you name the players who hold this somewhat dubious honor?

35) Twenty-two players who were with the Leafs during the 1960s, 1970s, 1980s or 1990s were eventually elected to the Hockey Hall of Fame. Can you name all of them (as of 2003)?

Hap Day and Harry Watson

36) Doug Gilmour holds the Leafs club record for most points in one season. Gilmour picked up 127 points during the 1992–93 season. Which player holds the second-highest total and how many points did he score?

37) Which Leaf holds the club record for most points and most goals in a season by a defenceman?

38) Which three players formed the highest-scoring line in Toronto Maple Leafs history?
Hint: All three players would be traded away to other teams.

39) The goaltender who holds the Leafs team record for the most career assists by a goaltender (16) once held the NHL record for

Leafs goaltender Harry Lumley gets help from Tim Horton (#7) to thwart the Boston Bruins attack.

most assists by a goaltender in one season (eight, in 1980–81). He set the latter record with another team. Who is he?

40) One player holds the Toronto Maple Leafs career records for most goals (389) and most points (916). Who is he and whose records did he break?

41) One player holds the Leafs team records for most seasons played (20) and most games played (1,187). Can you name him?

42) Which Leafs player holds the club record for most points in one season by a right winger? *Hint: He was acquired in a trade.*

43) The Leafs club record for most career penalty minutes is 1,948. The player who holds the mark also led the team in penalty minutes for seven straight seasons between 1995–96 and 2001–02. Can you name him?

44) The Leafs team record for most consecutive games played is held by a former defenceman who played in 486 straight contests. The

Brit Selby (#11) hopes for a rebound in front of the Boston net.

streak started on February 11, 1961, and ended on February 4, 1968. Can you name this durable Leaf?

45) The 1984–85 season is one the Toronto Maple Leafs organization would just as soon forget. This Leafs team set a new club record for futility. Can you name the record that was set and the mark it stands at?

46) Roger Neilson's style of coaching was widely criticized by many, especially in his second year with the team, 1978–79. However, in the spring of 1978 when the Leafs knocked off the New York Islanders in the playoffs, there were few dissenting voices to be heard. In fact, the Neilson team of 1977–78 tied a team record that previously had been set in 1950–51. Can you name the record the 1977–78 team tied? (It has since been surpassed.)

47) The club record for most goals allowed in one season by a Leafs team stands at 387. In which year did this happen?

48) The Maple Leafs team record for the longest losing streak is 10 games. Can you name the year in which this record was set?
Hint: There is a great irony involved when one considers the year this happened.

49) In the first game of the 1963 Stanley Cup finals versus Detroit, a Leaf winger set a playoff record by scoring the fastest two goals

Tim Horton

Defenceman Borje Salming (#21) is watched closely by Peter Mahovlich of Detroit.

from the start of the game and period—at 49 seconds and at 1:08 of the first period. The Leafs won the game 4–2 and went on to win the Stanley Cup in five games. Can you name the player who scored the record-setting goals?
Hint: He was later traded by the Leafs to the New York Rangers and went on to play for the Montreal Canadiens, the Los Angeles Kings and the Buffalo Sabres.

50) The Conn Smythe Trophy has been awarded annually since 1965 to the best playoff performer. The first player to win it two years in a row was a former Maple Leaf. Can you name him?

51) During 1960–61 to 1965–66, one Leaf led the team every season in goals scored. Six consecutive years leading the team in goal scoring is still a club record. This player also led the Leafs in total points scored in four of those six years and was tied for points leadership in another. Can you name him?

52) Only three players have scored more than 300 goals as members of the Maple Leafs. All three players were with the Leafs during the 1970s. Can you name them?

53) Which Leaf holds the team record for most career goals scored by a defenceman? Who held the record previously?

Hall of Fame defencemen Tim Horton and Allan Stanley

54) Ten Leafs have scored more than 200 goals (but less than 300) during their careers with Toronto. Can you name them?

55) Who holds the Leafs team record for most career points by a defenceman? Who held the record previously?

56) Ten players who at some point played with the Leafs have scored more than 1,000 points in their NHL careers. Can you name all 10 players?

57) Which two Leafs share the team record for most consecutive games with at least one point?

58) The Toronto Maple Leafs organization had one member elected to the Hockey Hall of Fame in the Builders section in 1965 and another in 1977. Can you name the two individuals to receive this honor?

59) The J.P. Bickell Memorial Cup, a Maple Leafs team trophy awarded at the discretion of the board of directors, was first given out in 1953. It has not been awarded every year, nor has it always gone to a player. Can you name the

Bickell winners between 1960 and 1972?
Hint: There are seven players to be named.

60) Since 1972, the J.P. Bickell Memorial Cup (see question 59) has been awarded only five times. Can you name all the recipients?

61) Which two players are tied for the most seasons (eight) leading the team in regular-season scoring?
Hint: Both players are centres.

62) A former Leafs goaltender holds the NHL record for the longest undefeated streak by a goalie. It was set in 1971–72 when he won 24 and tied 8 for a total of 32 games unbeaten. Can you name him?

63) On April 12, 1979, during the second game of the preliminary round playoff series against the Atlanta Flames, the Leafs set a new NHL playoff record for scoring. The record involves the first three goals of the game. What is the record and who scored the goals?

64) Dave Reid tied a Leafs team record in 1990–91 when he scored eight shorthanded goals in one season. Which Leaf established the previous mark?

Leafs captain Darryl Sittler had many great battles with Philadelphia Flyers leader Bobby Clarke.

65) The Molson Cup, given to the Leafs player who receives the most three-star selections during the entire season, has been awarded since the 1973–74 season. From 1973–74 through to 1979–80, only two players won the award. Can you name them?

66) Howie Meeker set a record for Leafs rookies in 1946–47 by scoring 27 goals. During the 1982–83 season, Walt Poddubny and Peter Ihnacak both broke the record and ended up tied at the end of the season with 28 goals each. In 1985–86 the record was broken by a rookie winger. Who is the new record holder?

67) Three players are tied for the Maple Leafs club record for most appearances on the NHL first and second All-Star Teams. Who are the players and how many times have they been named All-Stars?

68) In 1972, Bobby Orr set a new record for most points in a playoff year by a defenceman. Which Leafs rearguard held this record prior to Orr?

69) A former Maple Leaf holds the NHL record for the most career penalty minutes in both the regular season and playoffs. Who is he? *Hint: He has also played in Vancouver, Detroit and Los Angeles.*

70) Which player holds the record for most points and assists in one playoff year by a Maple Leaf?

Lanny McDonald loses his helmet along the boards.

71) Which player holds the Maple Leafs record for most goals in one playoff year?

72) In each of 1980–81, 1985–86 and 1989–90, the Leafs had four players score more than 30 goals, establishing the club record for the most 30-goal scorers in one season. Who are the four players from each of those three teams?

73) How many times since 1927 have the Leafs finished with the worst overall record in the NHL?

74) Since 1926–27, how many times have the Maple Leafs missed the playoffs?

75) Only 11 Maple Leafs players have scored 40 goals or more in one season. Can you name them?
Hint: No one Leaf scored more than 40 goals in any year prior to 1960–61.

76) Two Leafs have scored 50 or more goals since Rick Vaive first did it three years in a row between 1981 and 1984. Can you name the two wingers who joined Vaive in this exclusive club?

77) The shortest overtime playoff game the Leafs were ever involved in was on April 9, 1936, when Buzz Boll scored after just 31 seconds in a 4–3 Toronto semi-final win over Detroit at Maple Leaf Gardens. The second-shortest overtime game in Leafs history was also at the Gardens, on April 11, 1980, when Minnesota defeated Toronto 4–3 after just 32 seconds of extra play. Who scored the goal for the North Stars and who was the Leafs goalie?

Dave "Tiger" Williams rubs out the opposition.

78) Which Leafs player has captained the team to the most Stanley Cups, and how many?

79) Frank Mahovlich, Phil Esposito, Stan Mikita and Guy Lafleur each scored their 500th NHL goal against one-time Leafs goal-tenders. Can you name the goalies who allowed these milestone goals?
Hint: Mahovlich scored against Vancouver; Esposito against Detroit; Mikita against Vancouver; and Lafleur against New Jersey.

80) Who holds the Maple Leafs club record for most 20-goal seasons, and how many?

81) Who holds the Maple Leafs record for most 30-goal seasons, and how many?

82) Which Leaf holds the club record for the most consecutive games scoring at least one goal?

83) Which player holds the Leafs record for the fastest three goals in one game?

Dave Keon (#14) moves in on California netminder Gilles Meloche.

84) Which Leafs centre scored an assist in 12 consecutive games in the 1970–71 season?

85) Who was the first Maple Leafs player to score 20 goals or more in six consecutive seasons?

86) Who was the first Toronto Maple Leaf to
a) score 20 goals in one season?
b) score 30 goals in one season?
c) score 40 goals in one season?

87) Frank Mahovlich held the Maple Leafs record for the most goals in one season when he scored 48 in 1960–61. Rick Vaive broke the record in 1981–82. He scored his 49th goal to break the Big M's record on March 22, 1982, at Maple Leaf Gardens. Who was the opposition and who was the goalie?

88) Rick Vaive was the first Leaf to score 50 goals in one season. In fact, he did it three times, the first time in 1981–82 when he scored 54. Which goalie allowed Vaive's first 50th goal?

89) Who were the other two goalies to give up Rick Vaive's 50th goal?
Hint: They have the same first name.

90) When Frank Mahovlich set his record of 48 goals in one season in 1960–61, whose record did he break, and what was the previous record holder's goal total?

Rick Vaive (#22) scores another goal for the Leafs.

Gary Leeman

91) The record for most career shutouts in the playoffs is held by Patrick Roy with 23. Four goalies who have played with the Leafs have recorded at least 12 post-season shutouts. Can you name all four netminders?
Hint: Two of the goalies did not record a playoff shutout with Toronto.

92) Which Maple Leafs player holds the club record for most 40-goal seasons and how many did he record?

93) Which player holds the Maple Leafs team record for most points in one season by a left winger?

94) Which players hold the Maple Leafs team records for most career points by the following positions:
a) centre?
b) right wing?
c) left wing?

95) What is the most points a Leafs team has achieved in one season?

Dave Andreychuk

96) What is the fewest points a Leafs team has achieved in one season?

97) What is the Maple Leafs team record for fewest wins in one season?

98) What is the Maple Leafs record for fewest losses in one season?

99) What are the Leafs club records for most wins and most losses at home in one season?

100) What are the Leafs club records for most wins and most losses on the road in one season?

101) Which Leafs player was named to the NHL's All-Rookie Team, and won the *Sporting News* Rookie of the Year award (selected by the players) and the *Hockey News* Rookie of the Year award (selected by the fans) for his performance in 1985–86?

102) On December 29, 1988, in a game in Quebec against the Nordiques, the Leafs set a team record by scoring two goals four seconds apart. Which players scored the goals?

103) Which two players rank first and second in all-time Leafs playoff points?

Doug Gilmour

Felix Potvin

Darcy Tucker

104) The 1992–93 season was one of the most successful in Maple Leafs history, with 99 points and an appearance in the conference finals. Two members of that team won major awards at the end of the season. Can you name them and the trophies they earned?

105) In 1992–93, this first-year Leaf finished third in the voting for the Calder Trophy and was named to the NHL's All-Rookie Team. He also led the entire league with a 2.50 goals-against average. Can you name him?

106) Acquired in a trade from New York in exchange for Mathieu Schneider, this Leafs defenceman was an NHL-leading plus 39 during the 1998–99 season. Can you name him?

107) With a stellar performance during the 2002–03 season, Toronto's Ed Belfour shattered the club mark for most wins in a season by a netminder with 37 victories. Whose record did he break?

108) Drafted 256th overall by the Leafs in 1994, this Russian-born winger led the team in goals during the 1998–99 season, when he had 37 markers. Can you name him?

109) Picked up in a deal with Tampa Bay for winger Mike Johnson, this Leaf tied a club record on March 6, 2000, with two short-handed goals in one game against Vancouver. Can you name him?

Pat Quinn's first season behind the Leafs bench was in 1998–99.

Tie Domi (#28) in one of his many scraps.

110) Which former Leafs player holds the NHL record (as of the end of the 2002–03 season) for most overtime-winning goals in the regular season?

111) Which player holds the Toronto team record for the fastest goal (six seconds) from the start of an overtime period in the regular season?

112) During the 2001–02 season, Leafs goaltender Curtis Joseph faced a club-record-setting five penalty shots in one season. He was beaten only once, by a member of the Vancouver Canucks. Name the player that beat "Cujo."

113) Three players who were with the Maple Leafs at one point in their careers have won the King Clancy Memorial Trophy since its inception in 1988. The award is given to players who show exemplary leadership qualities on and off the ice and who have made significant humanitarian contributions to their community. Name all three.

114) At the end of the 2001–02 season, the Maple Leafs had a club member named to the NHL's second All-Star Team since 1979–80. Name the player.

115) When was the last time the Maple Leafs led the NHL in goal scoring?

Leafs captain Syl Apps is flanked by Hap Day (left) and Conn Smythe.

George Armstrong holds the 1963 Stanley Cup.

116) After leading the Leafs in points for eight straight seasons (1994–95 to 2001–02), Mats Sundin had his streak broken in 2002–03. Who was the Leafs leading point getter that year?

117) Name the three players who head the list of the Leafs' all-time penalty minute leaders.

118) Who is the only player in Leafs history to lead the team in assists for seven consecutive seasons (1995–96 to 2001–02)?

119) Which Leafs player was awarded the Lady Byng Trophy for his gentlemanly play during the 2002–03 season?

120) Can you name the four Maple Leafs coaches with the most career wins in the regular season (as of the end of 2002–03)?

Ed Olczyk (#16) and Gary Leeman (#11) storm the Quebec net.

Answers

1) Ace Bailey—1929; Harvey Jackson—1932; Charlie Conacher—1934 and 1935; Gord Drillon—1938
2) Turk Broda, Ted Kennedy and Don Metz
3) Ace Bailey (1928–29—22 goals); Charlie Conacher (1930–31—31 goals; 1931–32—34 goals; 1933–34—32 goals; 1934–35—36 goals; 1935–36—23 goals tied); Bill Thoms (1935–36—23 goals tied); Gord Drillon (1937–38—26 goals); Gaye Stewart (1945–46—37 goals)
4) Harvey "Busher" Jackson was named four times (1931–32; 1933–34; 1934–35; 1936–37).
5) Turk Broda (1941 and 1948); Al Rollins (1951); Harry Lumley (1954)
6) Joe Primeau (1932); Gord Drillon (1938); Syl Apps (1942); Sid Smith (1952 and 1955)
7) Syl Apps (1937); Gaye Stewart (1943); Gus Bodnar (1944); Frank McCool (1945); Howie Meeker (1947); Frank Mahovlich (1958); Dave Keon (1961)
8) Hap Day coached the Leafs to five Stanley Cups. Punch Imlach coached four Cup-winning teams.
9) Babe Pratt (1944) and Ted Kennedy (1955)
10) Conn Smythe was the general manager for seven Cup wins and Punch Imlach for four.
11) True. The record is 131 goals allowed, set by Toronto in 1953–54 and tied by Montreal in 1955–56.
12) Ted Kennedy
13) Harvey Jackson scored four goals in one period on November 20, 1934, against the St. Louis Eagles in a 5–2 Toronto win.
14) Charlie Conacher
15) Four (1932–33; 1933–34; 1934–35; 1937–38)
16) 22
17) Charlie Conacher scored five goals against the New York Americans on January 19, 1932, in a game the Leafs won 11–3.
18) Syl Apps (1938–39 and 1941–42)

19) Harry Lumley (1953–54 and 1954–55) and Sid Smith (1954–55)
20) 10 games (set in 1993–94)
21) Babe Pratt had six assists on January 8, 1944, when Toronto beat Boston 12–3, and Doug Gilmour also had six helpers against Minnesota on February 13, 1993, in a 6–1 win.
22) 11 games—from October 15, 1950, to November 8, 1950 (eight wins and three ties)
23) Turk Broda with 62 shutouts
24) Kent Douglas
25) Dave Keon
26) Brit Selby
27) Terry Sawchuk
28) Red Kelly in 1961; Dave Keon won the award in 1962 and 1963.
29) Jacques Plante, Borje Salming, Dave Keon, Darryl Sittler and Lanny McDonald. Salming made the first team in 1976–77.
30) Johnny Bower, Allan Stanley, Tim Horton, Carl Brewer, Frank Mahovlich and Dave Keon. Bower, Brewer, Horton and Mahovlich each made the first team at least once.
31) John McLellan for the 1970–71 season
32) It was Sawchuk's 100th NHL career shutout.
33) Tim Horton, George Armstrong, Dave Keon, Ron Ellis and Borje Salming
34) Carl Brewer for the 1959–60 and 1964–65 seasons, Forbes Kennedy in 1968–69 (he played part of the year for Philadelphia) and Dave "Tiger" Williams for the 1976–77 and 1978–79 seasons.
35) Johnny Bower, Terry Sawchuk, Jacques Plante, Tim Horton, Pierre Pilote, Marcel Pronovost, Allan Stanley, George Armstrong, Dickie Moore, Red Kelly, Andy Bathgate, Frank Mahovlich, Norm Ullman, Bert Olmstead, Bernie Parent, Dave Keon, Bob Pulford, Darryl Sittler, Lanny McDonald, Borje Salming, Mike Gartner and Grant Fuhr.

Toronto left winger Errol Thompson (#12) leads a rush.

Curtis Joseph

36) Darryl Sittler, with 117 points during the 1977–78 season, recorded the second-highest point total for Toronto.
37) In 1976–77 Ian Turnbull scored 22 goals and a total of 79 points to establish new club records for a defenceman. (Al Iafrate scored 22 goals in 1987–88.)
38) Centre Darryl Sittler (100 points), right winger Lanny McDonald (93 points) and left winger Errol Thompson (80 points) for a combined total of 273 points during 1975–76
39) Mike Palmateer (the NHL record has been surpassed)
40) Darryl Sittler, who surpassed Dave Keon's old records
41) George Armstrong
42) Wilf Paiement with 97 points in the 1980–81 season
43) Tie Domi
44) Tim Horton
45) The record set was most losses by a Leafs team during one season—52 (80-game schedule).
46) The 1977–78 team tied the Leafs team record for most wins in a season. They won 41 games in an 80-game schedule. The 1950–51 Leafs team won 41 games in a 70-game schedule. The 1998–99 and the 1999–2000 teams each won 45 games.
47) The year was 1983–84 when the Leafs finished 18th overall.
48) The streak for most consecutive losses started on January 15, 1967, and ended February 8, 1967. In April–May 1967, the Leafs won the Stanley Cup! (In 1987–88, the Leafs established a new mark by going 15 consecutive games without a win—11 losses and 4 ties.)
49) Dick Duff
50) Bernie Parent
51) Frank Mahovlich, who scored 48, 33, 36, 26, 23 and 32 goals to lead the Leafs in goals scored during each of these seasons.
52) Darryl Sittler, Dave Keon and Ron Ellis
53) Borje Salming scored 148 career goals—the most for a Leafs defenceman. Ian Turnbull held the previous record with 112 goals.
54) Mats Sundin (299), George Armstrong (296), Frank Mahovlich (296), Bob Pulford (251), Lanny McDonald (219), Rick Vaive (299), Wendel Clark (260), Ted Kennedy (231), Syl Apps (201), Charlie Conacher (200)
55) Borje Salming with 768 career points. This includes a club record of 620 career assists. Tim Horton held the mark previously with 458 points.
56) Norm Ullman, Frank Mahovlich, Darryl Sittler, Lanny McDonald, Glenn Anderson, Mike Gartner, Doug Gilmour, Larry Murphy, Dave Andreychuk, Mats Sundin
57) Darryl Sittler and Eddie Olczyk each scored a point in 18 consecutive games.
58) Foster Hewitt, long-time hockey broadcaster in 1965, and owner Harold Ballard in 1977
59) 1960—Johnny Bower; 1961—Red Kelly; 1962—Dave Keon; 1963—Dave Keon; 1964—Johnny Bower; 1965—Johnny Bower; 1966—Allan Stanley; 1967—Terry Sawchuk; 1968—no winner; 1969—Tim Horton; 1970—no winner; 1971—Bobby Baun; 1972—King Clancy (only non-player to win)
60) Mike Palmateer (1979), Doug Gilmour (1993), Bob Davidson (1995), Mats Sundin and Curtis Joseph (1999) and Pat Quinn (2002)
61) Darryl Sittler and Mats Sundin
62) Gerry Cheevers
63) The three Leafs' goals were scored within 23 seconds in the first period, setting a record for the fastest three goals by a team in the playoffs. Darryl Sittler scored the first two; Ron Ellis got the other. The Leafs won the game 7–4 and the series 2–0.
64) Dave Keon set the mark with eight shorthanded goals in 1970–71.
65) Borje Salming won it four times. Darryl Sittler won it three times.
66) Wendel Clark scored 34 goals as a rookie.
67) Borje Salming (1st team—once; 2nd team—five times); Tim Horton (1st team—three times; 2nd team—three times); Frank Mahovlich (1st team—twice; 2nd team—four times) have each been named All-Stars six times. Salming was selected in six consecutive years (1974–75 to 1979–80), as was Frank Mahovlich (1960–61 to 1965–66).
68) Tim Horton held the record for 10 years when he had 3 goals and 13 assists during the 1962 playoffs.
69) Dave "Tiger" Williams
70) Doug Gilmour had 35 points in the 1993 playoffs. He recorded 25 assists.
71) Dave Andreychuk scored 12 goals in 1993.

Wendel Clark was named captain of the Leafs in 1991.

72) In 1980–81: Darryl Sittler (43 goals); Wilf Paiement (40 goals); Bill Derlago (35 goals); Rick Vaive (33 goals)
In 1985–86: Wendel Clark (34 goals); Rick Vaive (33 goals); Miroslav Frycer (32 goals); Tom Fergus (31 goals)
In 1989–90: Gary Leeman (51 goals); Daniel Marois (39 goals); Vince Damphousse (33 goals); Eddie Olczyk (32 goals)
73) Twice (1957–58 and 1984–85)
74) 13
75) Rick Vaive, Bill Derlago, Darryl Sittler, Wilf Paiement, Lanny McDonald, Errol Thompson, Frank Mahovlich, Ed Olczyk, Wendel Clark, Dave Andreychuk and Mats Sundin
76) Gary Leeman (51 in 1989–90) and Dave Andreychuk (53 in 1993–94)
77) Al MacAdam beat goalie Jiri Crha.
78) George Armstrong—four
79) Frank Mahovlich—Dunc Wilson;
Phil Esposito—Jim Rutherford;
Stan Mikita—Cesare Maniago;
Guy Lafleur—Ron Low
80) Ron Ellis—11
81) Darryl Sittler—8
82) John Anderson scored in 10 consecutive games in 1984–85.
83) Lanny McDonald scored three goals in two minutes and 54 seconds on October 16, 1976, in a 5–5 tie against Philadelphia at the Gardens in the first period.
84) Norm Ullman
85) Sid Smith in the years 1949–50 to 1954–55
86) a) Bill Carson in 1927–28
b) Charlie Conacher in 1930–31
c) Frank Mahovlich in 1960–61
87) Toronto defeated the Chicago Blackhawks 8–5. Tony Esposito was the goalie.
88) Mike Liut (who was with the St. Louis Blues at the time) on March 24, 1982, in a 4–3 Toronto win
89) Gilles Gilbert (with Detroit); Gilles Meloche (with Minnesota)
90) Gaye Stewart (1945–46) and Tod Sloan (1955–56) held the mark prior to Mahovlich with 37 goals.
91) Curtis Joseph (15), Jacques Plante (14), Turk Broda (13) and Terry Sawchuk (12). Plante and Sawchuk did not record a playoff shutout with the Leafs.
92) Darryl Sittler—four (1975–76; 1977–78; 1979–80; 1980–81)
93) Dave Andreychuk recorded 99 points in 1993–94.
94) a) centre—Darryl Sittler (916)
b) right wing—George Armstrong (713)
c) left wing—Frank Mahovlich (597)
95) 100 points in 1999–2000 and in 2001–02 (82-game schedule, including points for regulation-time ties)
96) 48 points in 1984–85 (80-game schedule)
97) 20 (done twice in 1981–82 and 1984–85—both 80-game schedules)
98) 16 (set in 1950–51—70-game schedule)
99) Most wins—25 in 1961–62 (in 35 games)
Most wins—25 in 1992–93 (in 42 games)
Most losses—28 in 1984–85 (in 40 games)
100) Most wins—22 in 1998–99 (in 41 games)
Most losses—29 in 1983–84 (in 40 games)
Most losses—29 in 1972–73 (in 39 games)
101) Wendel Clark

102) Eddie Olczyk and Gary Leeman
103) Doug Gilmour (77 points) and Dave Keon (67 points)
104) Doug Gilmour won the Selke Trophy (best defensive forward) and Pat Burns won the Adams Award (as the league's best coach).
105) Felix Potvin
106) Alexander Karpovtsev (His mark was not officially recognized because he did not play in enough games to qualify for the NHL's award.)
107) Curtis Joseph previously held the mark at 36 wins, a record he set in 1999–2000.
108) Sergei Berezin
109) Darcy Tucker
110) Steve Thomas with 13 overtime winners
111) Mats Sundin, for a goal scored against St. Louis on December 30, 1995.
112) Markus Naslund
113) Lanny McDonald (1988), Kris King (1996) and Curtis Joseph (2000)
114) Mats Sundin
115) During the 1998–99 season, the Leafs led the NHL with 268 goals scored. The New Jersey Devils were second with 248.
116) Alex Mogilny lead the Leafs with 79 points in 2002–03.
117) Tie Domi (1,948 penalty minutes), Dave "Tiger" Williams (1,670) and Wendel Clark (1,535)
118) Mats Sundin
119) Alex Mogilny, who registered only 12 penalty minutes.
120) Punch Imlach (365 wins), Hap Day (259 wins), Dick Irvin (216 wins), Pat Quinn (214 wins)

Pat Burns is the only Maple Leafs coach to win the Jack Adams Award.

3

Trades

1) One of the most colourful people ever associated with the Maple Leafs is Francis "King" Clancy. The Leafs traded for Clancy in 1930 and he was a key player on the championship team of 1931–32. Leafs manager Conn Smythe sent two players and a large sum of money to

Frank Mahovlich

Ted Kennedy was one of the best Leafs captains in team history.

another team to obtain Clancy. Who were the two players, how much money was involved and who was the other team?

2) In 1939, Conn Smythe made one of his famous deals to acquire one great player. However, in this trade with the New York Americans, Smythe gave up one of the greatest Leafs ever—Harvey Jackson. Along with Jackson, four other players went to New York in exchange for one player. Who were the other players Smythe traded and who was the player the Leafs received in return?

3) Wally Stanowski and Elwyn "Moe" Morris were key members of the Leafs Cup-winning team in 1945. Both players would be dealt to the New York Rangers in 1948 to acquire a needed centreman and a tough defenceman. Who did the Leafs receive in this trade?

4) In 1943 the Maple Leafs made one of their greatest trades ever by sending defenceman Frank Eddols to the Montreal Canadiens. Who did the Leafs receive in return?

5) Although the Maple Leafs won the Stanley Cup in 1947, Conn Smythe traded away five players from that championship team to the Chicago Blackhawks. Although the Leafs received two players in return, Smythe was most concerned about getting one of the players in particular to strengthen the centre position. The centre Smythe wanted was a

slick play-maker who won the NHL scoring title two years in a row while with Chicago. As a Blackhawk, he also won the Hart Trophy and the Lady Byng Trophy. He helped Toronto to three Stanley Cups. Can you name the centre and the other player the Leafs received in the trade? Who were the five players they gave up?

Max Bentley ("A" on sweater) scores against Detroit's Terry Sawchuk.

6) During his NHL career, Eddie Shack had many stops in various cities, including two stints with the Maple Leafs. The Leafs acquired Eddie Shack in 1960 in a trade with the New York Rangers. The Leafs gave up two players to the Rangers in return for him. Can you name them?
Hint: One of the players became a colour commentator for the Buffalo Sabres' television broadcasts while the other became an NHL coach for various teams.

7) One of the best trades the Leafs ever made involved the acquisition of Red Kelly from the Detroit Red Wings. Can you name the player the Leafs gave the Red Wings in return for Kelly?

8) Allan Stanley played an integral role during the Leafs' championship years, the 1960s. Stanley and Tim Horton formed a formidable defensive combination. To acquire Stanley, the Leafs made a trade with the Boston Bruins. Can you name the player the Leafs traded away in exchange for the veteran blueliner?

9) While the Leafs were on their way to winning their third consecutive Stanley Cup in 1964, they made a major trade that Punch Imlach believed the team needed if it was to retain the Cup. The trade made on February 22, 1964, with the New York Rangers, had the Leafs giving up five players in exchange for two. Can you name all seven players involved?

10) After gaining All-Star status and playing on four Stanley Cup–winning teams with the Detroit Red Wings, Marcel Pronovost was traded to Toronto in the spring of 1965 and

made a major contribution to the Leafs' Cup victory in 1967. Pronovost was traded along with four other players, two of whom participated in the 1967 championship year with Toronto. The Leafs gave up three players in return. Can you name the eight players involved in the transaction?

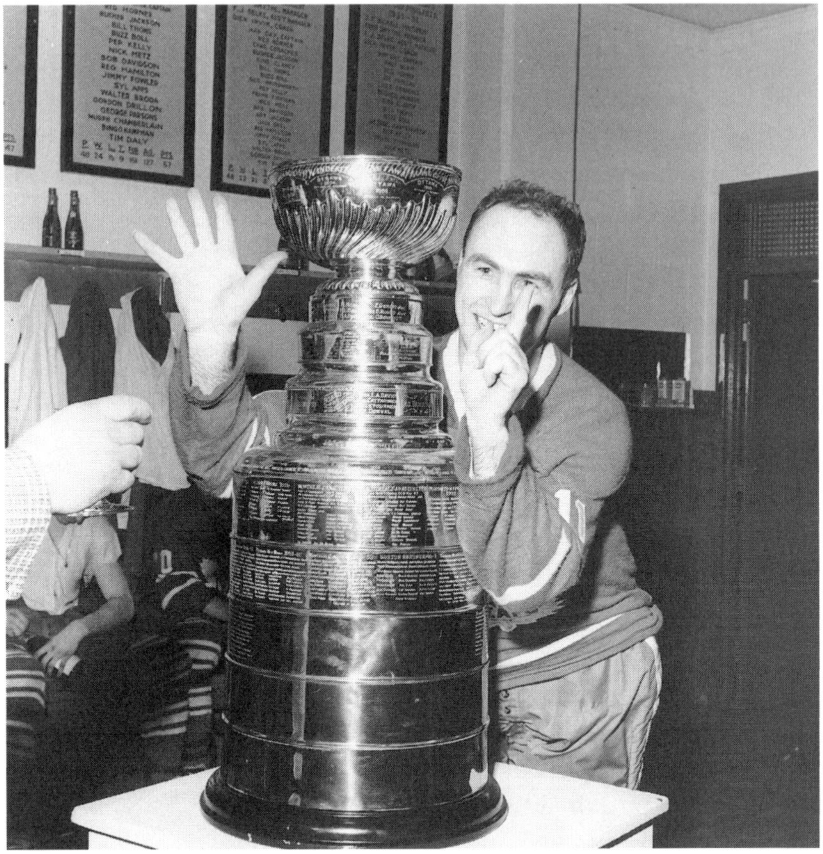

Red Kelly and the 1963 Stanley Cup, the sixth of his career

11) After playing 13 seasons on three Stanley Cup teams with the Leafs, right winger Ron Stewart was traded to the Boston Bruins in 1965 in exchange for three players. Can you name them? *Hint: One of the players was a former NHL iron man who once held the record for most consecutive games played. Another would later coach the Vancouver Canucks, and the third player went on to a great career with the Chicago Blackhawks and played on Team Canada in 1972. Of the three players acquired, only one actually played for the Leafs.*

12) In June 1967, the Los Angeles Kings traded unknown defenceman Ken Block to Toronto for the rights to a player who had helped the Leafs win the Stanley Cup earlier that year. Who was that player and in what capacity was he used in the Kings' first NHL season?

13) One of the most controversial trades the Leafs ever made involved the Big M, Frank Mahovlich, who was traded to Detroit. The main acquisition for the Leafs in this trade with the Red Wings in March 1968 was centre Norm Ullman. Can you name all the other players involved from both teams?

14) Perhaps one of the worst trades ever made by the Leafs involved Jim Pappin. Despite playing a vital role in helping the Leafs in the Stanley Cup in 1967, his disagreements with Punch Imlach led to a trade to the Chicago Blackhawks, where he enjoyed many fine years. Can you name the player the Leafs

received in return for Pappin?
Hint: The player the Leafs acquired was a former Norris Trophy winner.

15) After the Leafs won the Stanley Cup in 1967, many changes occurred on the team for the following year, despite the victory. One was the trading of Eddie Shack to Boston. Can you name the player the Leafs received in return?
Hint: The player went on to play for Minnesota and later became an assistant coach with the North Stars. He also played with the Detroit Red Wings and scored 274 goals in his NHL career.

16) The Philadelphia Flyers claimed former rookie of the year Brit Selby from Toronto in the 1967 expansion draft. The Leafs re-acquired Selby, along with another player from Philadelphia, in March 1969 in

Allan Stanley (#26) battles with Gordie Howe of the Red Wings.

Tim Horton (#7) keeps his eye on the puck, and goalie Johnny Bower has Stan Mikita of Chicago to watch.

exchange for three players. Can you name all the players involved?

17) Bob Pulford had a very distinguished career as a Maple Leaf. He was certainly a vital part of the Stanley Cup championship teams of the 1960s, often scoring key goals in important games. However, in September 1970, he was traded by Toronto to the Los Angeles Kings, where he finished his active career as a player before turning to coaching. The Leafs received two players in exchange for Pulford. Can you name them?

18) After a long and illustrious career with the Leafs, Tim Horton was traded away for three players in 1970. Horton ended up with the New York Rangers in this trade that also involved the St. Louis Blues. Of the three players the Leafs received, one was a goaltender and two were forwards. Can you name them?

19) Former Leafs general manager Jim Gregory was often criticized for trades he made, but very few people quarrelled with the deal he made to get Bernie Parent from Philadelphia. Can you name the two players Gregory gave to the Flyers in exchange for Parent?

20) Near the end of the 1972–73 season the Leafs decided to unload veteran goaltender Jacques Plante in a trade with the Boston Bruins. The Bruins agreed to send the Leafs a first-round draft choice and a player to be named later. Can you name the player, and the draft choice?

21) When he first came to the Leafs, Rick Kehoe looked like a promising winger, especially when he scored 33 goals in 1972–73. However, the next season he slumped to 18 goals and claimed he did not get along with coach Red Kelly. After Kehoe asked to be traded, the Leafs sent him to Pittsburgh. Can you name the player the Leafs received in the trade? *Hint: In the 1979–80 season, this player scored 56 goals for a former WHA (World Hockey Association) team. He had originally left the Leafs to sign with Cincinnati of the WHA.*

Ron Ellis of the Leafs is checked by Paul Henderson (#19) of Detroit.

22) When Bernie Parent left the WHA in 1973, he did not want to play for Toronto, who still owned his NHL playing rights. Instead, he sought to return to Philadelphia. The Leafs accommodated both Parent and the Flyers by completing a trade. In return for Parent, the Leafs received a goaltender and a 1973 draft choice. Can you name the goaltender and the draft choice?

23) Doug Jarvis was the centreman on the Montreal Canadiens checking line, which was so vital to their string of four straight Stanley Cups from 1976 to 1979. The Leafs had actually made Jarvis their second-round selection in the 1975 amateur draft, but traded him away before he ever suited up for the Leafs. Who did Montreal give to Toronto in order to acquire Jarvis?

Bob Pulford

24) Randy Carlyle won the James Norris Trophy as the NHL's best defenceman for the 1980–81 season. Carlyle was once a Leaf for two seasons before he and another player were traded to the Pittsburgh Penguins in exchange for a defenceman. Can you name the other player the Leafs traded away with Carlyle, and the defenceman the Leafs received in return?

Bobby Hull of Chicago scores against goalie Bruce Gamble of the Leafs.

25) Despite having one of his finest seasons as a Leaf in 1977–78, this defenceman, who once captained the Toronto Marlies and who played for the Canadian National Team, was traded away along with two other Leafs to the Los Angeles Kings. In exchange, the Leafs received a defenceman better known for his toughness than his hockey skills, and a left winger who had played for the Marlies. Can you name all five players involved in this transaction? *Hint: Of the players the Leafs gave to the Kings, the defenceman was forced to retire two years later, one never played for L.A. and the other was killed in an auto accident. The two players the Leafs received would stay in Toronto less than two years.*

26) During the late stages of the 1978–79 season, the Leafs were desperately looking for a scoring centre to take pressure off Darryl Sittler. As a result, the Leafs made a deal with the Colorado Rockies for a sharp-scoring centre whose dad once played for the Maple Leafs. In order for the Leafs to acquire the centreman, they gave up two players—one centre and one defenceman. Who were the two they gave up?

27) Punch Imlach made numerous controversial trades involving the Leafs over his many years with the team—none more so than the trading of high-scoring and extremely popular Lanny McDonald to the Colorado Rockies. McDonald and another Leaf were sent to Denver in exchange for two forwards. Who was the other Leaf involved and who did Toronto acquire in the deal?

28) One of Punch Imlach's better trades in his second term as Leafs general manager was the deal that sent winger Reg Thomas to Quebec in exchange for a forward and a

defenceman. These two players performed well for Toronto when they were used. Can you name them?

29) Despite providing the Leafs with some fine goaltending, especially during the 1978 playoffs against the New York Islanders, the very popular Mike Palmateer was traded to the Washington Capitals for two players. Can you name them?
Hint: One was traded away less than one season later, while the other never played for Toronto.

30) The Leafs once made a trade for a goaltender mid-season and that goaltender won a share of the Vezina Trophy—with the other goaltenders of the team he was acquired from. Can you name this goaltender and the player the Leafs gave up to get him?
Hint: This goaltender had shared the Vezina Trophy on three other occasions, while the player the Leafs traded was the third player taken overall in the 1977 entry draft.

31) Punch Imlach's house cleaning in 1979–80 included the trading of unheralded checker Pat Boutette to the Hartford Whalers. In the 1980–81 season, Boutette scored 80 points in 80 games for Hartford, while the player the Leafs acquired in exchange did not play for

Goalie Bunny Laroque makes a save versus Keith Acton of the Canadiens.

Netminder Mike Palmateer discusses strategy with Dave Williams.

Toronto at all that season (and was a Leaf for just 14 games). Can you name the player the Leafs received from Hartford?

32) The first-round draft picks of the Vancouver Canucks for 1978 and 1979 were two players who eventually found themselves in Toronto via a trade that involved both of them. In order to obtain these two young players, the Leafs gave up a couple of veterans to the Canucks. Who were the two players the Leafs acquired and who were the two they traded away?

Dan Maloney (#9) was acquired from Detroit in a trade.

33) With their first pick of the 1969 amateur draft, Detroit selected a goaltender from the Hamilton Red Wings junior club. His first season with Detroit was 1970–71, when he appeared in 29 games. The following year he was claimed by Pittsburgh in the intra-league draft. He was subsequently dealt back to the Red Wings in January 1974. He stayed with Detroit until the 1980–81 season, when the Leafs acquired him for a young centre. His stay in Toronto was brief—he was traded away that same year. Can you name the goaltender, the player the Leafs gave up to get him and the team the Leafs dealt him to?

34) As part of the trade to acquire Dan Maloney from Detroit, the Leafs gave the Red Wings first- and second-round choices in the 1978

entry draft as well as a first-round pick in the 1980 draft. In addition to Maloney, the Leafs were given a second-round 1980 draft choice. Who did the Red Wings select with their choices and who did the Leafs take? *Hint: All three players the Red Wings picked were traded away by Detroit!*

Pat Boutette

35) Despite winning the Toronto version of the Molson Cup in 1981–82, goaltender Michel "Bunny" Larocque was traded away the following season to the Philadelphia Flyers for another goaltender. Who did the Leafs receive in exchange for Larocque?

36) After a final few controversial seasons in Toronto, the Leafs finally traded one of their best players ever—Darryl Sittler—in January 1982. The former captain was dealt to the Philadelphia Flyers for three players. Can you name them?

37) In June 1979, the Leafs made centre Laurie Boschman their number-one draft choice. Despite a somewhat promising rookie year in Toronto in which he scored 48 points, Boschman was never able to live up to his potential with the Leafs. He was traded to the Edmonton Oilers in March 1982. The Leafs received two players for Boschman. Can you name them?

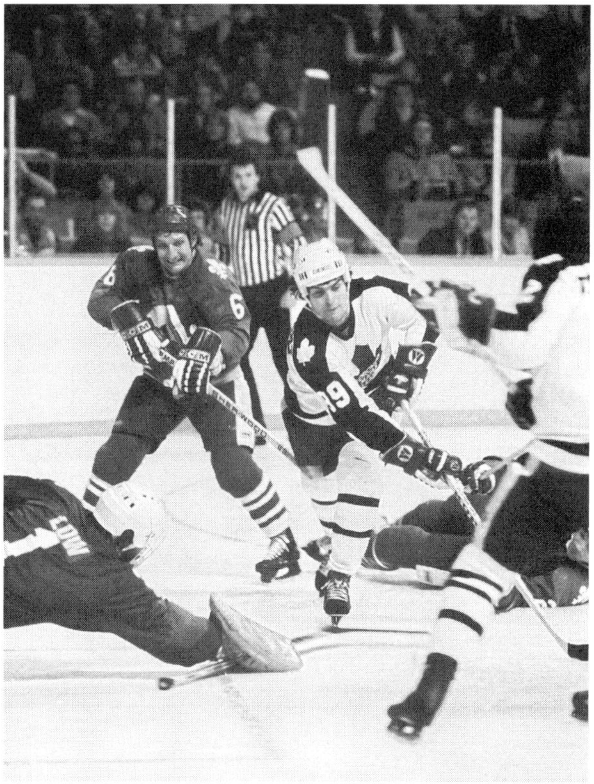

Wilf Paiement (#99) was obtained in a deal with Colorado.

38) In March 1982, the Leafs completed a trade with the Quebec Nordiques, acquiring Czechoslovakian right winger Miroslav Frycer, who had been signed by Quebec as a free agent. Along with Frycer, the Leafs were given a seventh-round draft choice. Who did the Leafs give up in return?
Hint: The Leafs had acquired this right winger in a trade two years earlier.

39) Acquired from the Montreal Canadiens in December 1982 for a third-round draft choice, this centre was named to the NHL All-Rookie Team after playing in only 48 games and scoring 51 points. Can you name him?

40) After spending his entire career in the Maple Leafs organization, John Anderson was traded away to the Quebec Nordiques prior to the 1985–86 season. In exchange, Toronto received a defenceman who was Minnesota's first-round draft selection (seventh overall) in 1977. Can you name him?

41) Just after the start of the 1985–86 season, the Leafs completed a one-for-one trade with the Boston Bruins. Both players were centres. Can you name both players?

Master trader Cliff Fletcher

42) Born in Czechoslovakia, defenceman Rick Lanz was the first draft choice of the Vancouver Canucks in 1980. He was acquired by the Leafs in 1986 for two players. The Leafs sent a defenceman and a centre to Vancouver to complete the deal. Can you name the two players?

43) The Leafs acquired left winger Mark Osborne, who started his career in Detroit and later played for the New York Rangers, on March 3, 1987, in exchange for another left winger and a third-round draft choice. Who was the player Toronto gave to the Rangers?

Dave Ellett

Peter Zezel

44) Prior to the 1987–88 season, the Leafs sent defenceman Bill Root to Hartford. In exchange, Toronto received a tough winger who had played on two Stanley Cup–winning teams with the Edmonton Oilers, where he protected superstar Wayne Gretzky. He also scored the last goal in the history of the WHA. Who is he?

45) One of the few Canadian university (Acadia) players to make it to the NHL, this defenceman was acquired by the Leafs from Hartford in exchange for winger Stewart Gavin. Who is he?

46) In September 1986, the Chicago Blackhawks signed Leafs defenceman Gary Nylund as a free agent. However, because of NHL compensation rules, Chicago had to reach an agreement with Toronto as to who would be sent to the Leafs in return. When an agreement could not be reached, both teams submitted a proposal to an arbitrator who would pick one solution. The ruling went in favour of Chicago because their offer was judged to be fairest. Which players ended up coming to Toronto and who was the player the Leafs had sought?

47) In one of the biggest trades ever made, Toronto sent former captain Rick Vaive, winger Steve Thomas and defenceman Bob McGill to Chicago in exchange for two players on September 3, 1987. What two players did Toronto obtain?

48) In his first trade as the Leafs' new general manager, Gord Stellick sent disgruntled winger Miroslav Frycer to Detroit in exchange for a defenceman. The player the Leafs acquired was a former first-round draft selection of the Washington Capitals (fifth overall in 1980). Who is he?

Grant Fuhr

Todd Gill

Rob Ramage (#8) came to the Leafs in an off-season trade.

49) Acquired from the Calgary Flames in exchange for a second-round draft choice, this defenceman would be named captain of the Leafs before he wore the sweater even one time. Can you name him?

50) In one of the most ridiculous trades ever made by the Maple Leafs, a 1991 first-round draft choice (which turned out to be third overall) was sent to the New Jersey Devils (who selected Scott Niedermayer) in exchange for a defenceman who stayed in Toronto for just a couple of seasons. Name him.
Hint: He was a member of the 1986 Montreal Canadiens Stanley Cup-winning team.

51) One of the better deals the Leafs completed took place on November 10, 1990, when the team acquired a quality defenceman from Winnipeg in return for forwards Eddie Olczyk and Mark Osborne. Toronto also received a forward in the deal. Who were the two players the Leafs received in the trade?

52) The Leafs finally gave up on the great enigma known as Al Iafrate when they dealt the defenceman to Washington in return for two players on January 16, 1991. Both the players the Leafs received made great contributions to the team during their stays in Toronto. Can you name them?

53) The first major deal made in the Cliff Fletcher era was with Edmonton on September 19, 1991, when the Leafs' new general manager picked up Oilers stars Grant Fuhr and Glenn Anderson along with Craig Berube. What four players did the Leafs send to Edmonton?

54) Doug Gilmour, Jamie Macoun, Kent Manderville and Rick Wamsley were acquired by the Maple Leafs from the Calgary Flames on January 2, 1992, in the largest regular-season deal in NHL history. Who did the Leafs send out west to complete the trade?

Defenceman Bryan McCabe came to the Leafs from Chicago.

55) Winger Daniel Marois scored more than 30 goals twice in his career with the Leafs, but he was dealt away, with another player, to the New York Islanders. The Leafs received two forwards in the deal. Can you name the three players, aside from Marois, involved in this transaction?

56) In one of the best deals the Leafs ever made, a third-round draft choice was sent to the Montreal Canadiens in August 1992 for an unknown blueliner. Name him.
Hint: This defenceman won a Stanley Cup with Colorado in 1996.

57) When Felix Potvin became the Leafs' number-one goaltender, the Leafs had no

Aki Berg was originally a high draft choice of the Los Angeles Kings.

room for Grant Fuhr. The veteran goalie was sent to Buffalo for a big winger, a goaltender and a number-one draft choice. Name all three players the Leafs received in this deal.

58) In a transaction that was made because Cliff Fletcher wanted to complete a deal at the trade deadline, the Leafs sent Glenn Anderson, Scott Malone and a fourth-round draft choice to the New York Rangers in exchange for what player?

59) In a shocking deal completed on June 28, 1994, with the Quebec Nordiques, the Leafs sent Wendel Clark, Sylvain Lefebvre, Landon Wilson and a switch of number-one draft choices to the Nordiques in return for which players?

60) A two-time winner of the Stanley Cup with Pittsburgh, All-Star defenceman Larry Murphy was acquired by Toronto in exchange for another blueliner. Murphy's stay in Toronto was not a happy one and he was eventually moved to Detroit where he won two more Cups. The player the Leafs gave up to get Murphy ended up in Detroit at one point and shared in the 1998 Red Wing championship. Can you name him?

61) Todd Gill was a loyal Maple Leaf (with the team from 1984 to 1996) who finally played some good hockey when he got the proper coaching (and when paired with Dave Ellett). Although he was prone to making some costly errors at times, Gill was also very steady and would stand up for many a teammate. In one of the worst deals made by Cliff Fletcher, the defenceman was sent to San Jose for what player?

62) In 1997, Doug Gilmour let it be known that he wanted to be traded, and the Leafs accommodated him with a move to the New Jersey Devils on February 25, 1997. The Leafs received three players in return. Can you name all three?

63) When the Leafs signed Curtis Joseph in the summer of 1998 to play in goal, it meant that Felix Potvin had to be traded away. It took a while (until January 9, 1999), but associate general manager Mike Smith finally sent the netminder to the New York Islanders in exchange for which defenceman?

MARCEL PRONOVOST

64) Fredrik Modin showed a lot of promise (twice scoring 16 goals in a season), but when he could not be a consistent winger on the line centred by Mats Sundin, Leafs coach and general manager Pat Quinn sent the large winger to Tampa Bay in exchange for a defenceman. Can you name him?

65) When the Maple Leafs had trouble signing defenceman Alexander Karpovtsev, they quickly shipped him off to Chicago for another blueliner who was younger and about to become a quality player. Name him.

66) A former high draft choice of the Los Angeles Kings (third overall in 1995), defenceman Aki Berg was acquired by the Leafs in exchange for one player and a second-round draft choice in 2001. Name the player and who the draft choice turned out to be.

67) The Leafs acquired Mikael Renberg, a former member of Philadelphia's "Legion of Doom" line (along with Eric Lindros and John LeClair), from the Phoenix Coyotes in exchange for which Leafs winger?

68) Todd Warriner was never able to reach his potential with the Maple Leafs. They eventually got tired of waiting for this talented but enigmatic player to develop, and sent him in 2000 to Tampa Bay for a third-round draft choice that they used to select a goaltender. This goalie recorded his first win with the team on February 22, 2003, in Montreal. Name the netminder.

69) After the Leafs nearly lost him in a proposed deal with Philadelphia involving Eric Lindros, they foolishly traded defenceman Danny Markov to Phoenix for three players. The Leafs did receive one quality player, Travis Green, in the exchange, but the other two players who came to Toronto were a career minor leaguer and a centre who was supposed to anchor the second line. Name those two other players that Toronto received in the deal.

70) Leafs defenceman Dmitry Yushkevich was very upset when he was prevented from playing in the 2002 playoffs (supposedly by team lawyers, on account of a potentially dangerous blood clot). During the off-season he was dealt to Florida for another blueliner but not before he accused Leafs management of dishonesty. Who did the Leafs acquire in the deal?

71) This former Vezina Trophy winner (1984) and NHL rookie of the year (1984) was acquired by the Maple Leafs late in the

Goalie Jacques Plante talks it over with Paul Henderson.

Norm Ullman

2001–02 season from the Carolina Hurricanes as insurance for the netminding duties. His stay with the Leafs was relatively short. Name him.

72) Toronto signed defenceman Dave Manson (a former first-round choice of the Chicago Black Hawks) as a free agent in August of 2000. His stay with the Maple Leafs lasted just one season before he was dealt to Dallas for another veteran blueliner. Who did the Leafs receive in return?

73) After supposedly coming close a number of times, the Leafs finally pulled the trigger on a major swap in March of 2002 and acquired Owen Nolan from San Jose for a heavy price. Who did the Leafs give up in return?

74) In order to bolster the team prior to the 2003 playoffs, the Leafs added three veteran players in exchange for a number of draft choices. They added two defencemen and a forward who had once been a Leafs star. Name all three acquisitions.

Danny Markov was traded away to Phoenix.

Right winger Owen Nolan was acquired in a deal with San Jose.

Answers

1) Smythe sent Art Smith and Eric Pettinger to the Ottawa Senators along with $35,000.
2) Along with Harvey Jackson, the Leafs sent Murray Armstrong, Jim Fowler, Buzz Boll and Doc Romnes to New York in return for Dave "Sweeney" Schriner.
3) Cal Gardner and Bill Juzda
4) Ted Kennedy
5) Toronto acquired centre Max Bentley and Cy Thomas. In exchange, the Leafs sent Bob Goldham, Ernie Dickens, Gus Bodnar, Bud Poile and Gaye Stewart to Chicago.
6) Pat Hannigan and Johnny Wilson
7) Marc Reaume
8) Jim Morrison
9) The Leafs traded Bob Nevin, Dick Duff, Arnie Brown, Bill Collins and Rod Seiling in exchange for Andy Bathgate and Don McKenney.
10) Detroit sent Pronovost, Autry Erickson, Larry Jeffery, Ed Joyal and Lowell McDonald to the Leafs in return for Andy Bathgate, Billy Harris and Gary Jarrett.
11) The Leafs obtained Andy Hebenton, Orland Kurtenbach and Pat Stapleton.
12) Los Angeles obtained Red Kelly in the trade to be their first-ever coach.
13) The Leafs gave up Frank Mahovlich, Gary Unger, Pete Stemkowski, and the rights to Carl Brewer (then retired) in exchange for Norm Ullman, Paul Henderson and Floyd Smith.
14) Pierre Pilote
15) Murray Oliver
16) Along with Selby, Toronto obtained Forbes Kennedy in exchange for Mike Byers, Gerry Meehan and Bill Sutherland.
17) Garry Monahan and Brian Murphy

Brian Glennie (#24) was a terrific open-ice bodychecker.

18) Jacques Plante, Denis Dupere and Guy Trottier
19) Mike Walton and goaltender Bruce Gamble
20) The player was Eddie Johnston and the draft choice turned out to be Ian Turnbull.
21) Blaine Stoughton
22) Doug Favell and Bob Neely
23) Greg Hubick
24) George Ferguson went with Carlyle to the Penguins in exchange for Dave Burrows. Burrows was traded back to Pittsburgh during the 1980–81 season.
25) The Leafs traded Brian Glennie, Kurt Walker and Scott Garland (since deceased) to Los Angeles in exchange for Dave Hutchison and Lorne Stamler.
26) The Leafs acquired Paul Gardner from Colorado in exchange for Don Ashby and Trevor Johansen.
27) Lanny McDonald was traded along with Joel Quenneville to Colorado for Wilf Paiement and Pat Hickey.
28) Terry Martin and Dave Farrish
29) Robert Picard and Tim Coulis
30) The Leafs acquired Michel Laroque from Montreal in exchange for Robert Picard.
31) Bob Stephenson
32) The Leafs acquired Bill Derlago (Vancouver's first choice in 1978) and Rick Vaive (Vancouver's first choice in 1979), and traded away Dave "Tiger" Williams and Jerry Butler.
33) Goaltender Jim Rutherford was acquired by Toronto in exchange for centre Mark Kirton. The Leafs traded Rutherford to the Los Angeles Kings.
34) The Red Wings selected Brent Peterson and Al Jensen in 1978. Detroit took Mike Blaisdell in 1980. The Leafs selected Craig Muni in 1980.
35) Rick St. Croix
36) Peter Ihnacak, Ken Strong and Rich Costello
37) Walt Poddubny and Phil Drouilliard
38) Wilf Paiement
39) Dan Daoust
40) Brad Maxwell

Left winger Steve Thomas crashes the Edmonton net.

41) Toronto traded Bill Derlago to Boston in exchange for Tom Fergus.
42) Jim Benning and Dan Hodgson
43) Jeff Jackson
44) Dave Semenko
45) Chris Kotsopoulos
46) The Leafs received Jerome Dupont and Ken Yaremchuk. The player the Leafs asked for was Eddie Olczyk.
47) Al Secord and Eddie Olczyk
48) Darren Veitch
49) Rob Ramage
50) Tom Kurvers
51) Dave Ellett and Paul Fenton
52) Peter Zezel and Bob Rouse
53) Vince Damphousse, Luke Richardson, Scott Thornton and Peter Ing
54) Gary Leeman, Michel Petit, Jeff Reese, Craig Berube and Alexander Godynyuk
55) Ken Baumgartner and Dave McLlwain
56) Sylvain Lefebvre
57) Dave Andreychuk, Daren Puppa and Kenny Jonsson (selected in the entry draft)
58) Mike Gartner
59) Mats Sundin, Todd Warriner and Garth Butcher
60) Dmitri Mironov
61) Jamie Baker
62) Jason Smith, Steve Sullivan and Alyn McCauley
63) Bryan Berard
64) Cory Cross
65) Bryan McCabe
66) Adam Mair was the player, and Mike Cammalleri was selected by the Kings
67) Sergei Berezin
68) Mikael Tellqvist
69) Craig Mills and Robert Reichel
70) Robert Svehla
71) Tom Barrasso
72) Jyrki Lumme
73) Alyn McCauley, Brad Boyes and a first-round draft choice in 2003
74) Glen Wesley, Phil Housley and Doug Gilmour

4

Remember Him?

1) The first player to sign a contract with the new Toronto franchise named "Maple Leafs" in February 1927 was also the first United States-born player to play for the organization. He only played in nine games for the Leafs, but was rookie of the year in 1933 with Detroit and scored a Stanley Cup–winning goal for Chicago in 1938. Can you name him?

2) This Leafs defenceman led the NHL for a record eight consecutive seasons in penalty minutes (1932 to 1940). Can you name him?

3) The first Leafs goalie to backstop the team to a Stanley Cup (1931–32) was involved in a couple of hockey's greatest moments. For example, he was in net for the longest overtime game ever played (March 24, 1936), between the Montreal Maroons and the Detroit Red Wings. He was in goal for the Maroons when Mud Bruneteau beat him at 16:30 of the sixth overtime period—thus ending this playoff game at 2:25 a.m.! As well, this was the goalie that New York Rangers coach Lester Patrick replaced in a playoff game after the player suffered an injury. This marked the first and only time a coach started a game behind the bench and finished it in the net! Can you name the goalie in question?

4) The goalie who holds the NHL record for most shutouts in one season (22 in a 44-game season with the Montreal Canadiens) later went on to play for the Maple Leafs. This goalie also won the Vezina Trophy (with Montreal) the first three years it was awarded. Can you name him?

5) One of the few players in NHL history to score six goals in one game, this centre did it for the Detroit Red Wings on February 3, 1944, in a 12–2 victory over the New York Rangers. The player who accomplished this feat played with the Leafs in 1931–32. Can you name him?

6) The first-ever winner of two major NHL awards, the Hart Trophy and the Lady Byng Trophy, ended his career in 1929–30 with the Maple Leafs. This forward was also on four Stanley Cup teams (three with the Ottawa Senators and one with the Vancouver Millionaires) and was later elected to the Hockey Hall of Fame. Can you name him?

7) As a result of a stick injury suffered by a Leafs player in 1939 the NHL adopted a rule prohibiting players with vision in only one eye from playing in the league. Can you name the player whose accident led to this major rule change?

Goaltender Lorne Chabot

8) As an assistant to Conn Smythe, this man was with the Leafs for many years and played a large role in developing the Leafs farm system. Eventually he left Toronto and went to Montreal, where he was the team's manager during the Canadiens' five-year reign as Stanley Cup champions (1955–60). Today, an NHL award is named in his honor and is awarded to each season's best defensive forward. Can you name him?

9) Nicknamed "Flash," this defenceman gained more recognition while playing for the Detroit Red Wings than in his time with the Leafs. He set a record for defencemen in 1944–45 by scoring 20 goals in one season. The record stood until 1969, when it was broken by Bobby Orr. This player was also the only non–Montreal Canadien on the NHL first All-Star Team of 1944–45. Can you name him?

10) In the 1938 Stanley Cup finals, the Maple Leafs faced the Chicago Blackhawks. The first game was to be played in Toronto, but the Blackhawks' first-string goalie was injured with no backup available. In desperation Chicago went with an obscure minor leaguer who happened to be a Toronto native. In his first and last game of the series, this goalie turned back Toronto 3–1 and Chicago went on to win the Cup. Who was the goaltender?

11) Prior to the 1941–42 season, the Leafs sent four players to the New York Americans in exchange for a right winger. It proved to be an excellent deal because this winger made the NHL first All-Star Team twice (1942–43 and 1943–44) and also scored the most goals on the team for two years in a row. He was also on two Stanley Cup-winning teams with the Leafs. Can you name him?

William Hollett

12) A goaltender with the Maple Leafs during the 1945–46 season went on to become the general manager of the Pittsburgh Penguins in 1977. His hockey career was cut short due to an eye injury. In March 1983, he was killed in an auto accident. Can you name him?

13) Maurice "Rocket" Richard was one of the NHL's greatest playoff performers. Perhaps his best playoff game came against the Leafs on March 23, 1944, when he scored all five of Montreal's goals in a 5–1 semi-final game victory. Who was the Leafs' goaltender that night?

14) One of only four people to coach the Leafs to a Stanley Cup victory, this former centreman was behind the bench when Toronto won the championship in 1951. Can you name him?

15) Perhaps the greatest Leafs centre ever, this player won the Calder Trophy, the Lady Byng Trophy, and was the captain for three Stanley Cup teams. He was also very accomplished off the ice, representing Canada in the 1936 Olympic Games in track and field and serving in the army during the Second World War. After his retirement from hockey, he joined the Ontario government as the Conservative MP from Kingston. This Hockey Hall of Fame member had a son who played in the NHL with New York, Pittsburgh and Los Angeles. Can you name this great Leaf?

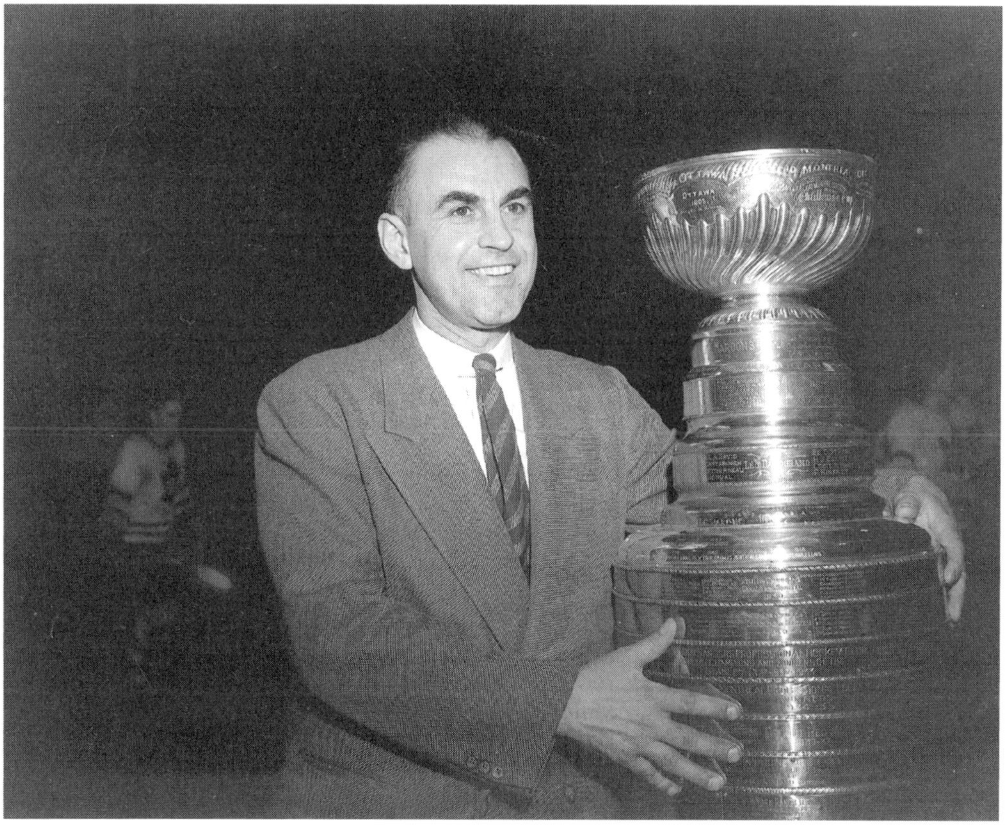

Joe Primeau with the Stanley Cup

Three great Leafs: (left to right) Ted Kennedy, Max Bentley and Syl Apps

16) This Leafs centre from Fort William, Ontario, set an NHL record for rookies by scoring just 15 seconds into his first NHL game in 1943. Years later, with the Chicago Blackhawks, he would be the centre for Bill Mosienko when the latter scored an NHL-record three goals in 21 seconds. Coincidentally, both records were set against the New York Rangers. Later he would coach the Toronto Marlboros to the Memorial Cup in 1967. Can you name him?

17) The captain of the 1944–45 Maple Leafs Stanley Cup–winning team later became Toronto's chief scout—a position he held for many years. His career with the Leafs spanned 10 years and he went on to coach the Toronto Marlboros. Can you name him?

18) During the 1940s, two brothers played together on four Maple Leafs Stanley Cup–winning teams. Can you name this brother act?

19) For the 1944–45 season, the Leafs' regular goaltender Turk Broda was away in Europe fighting in the Second World War. His replacement backstopped the Toronto team to a Stanley Cup victory in the finals against the Detroit Red Wings. In the first three games of the series, this goalie shut out Detroit 1–0, 2–0 and 1–0 for an NHL-record three consecutive shutouts in the playoffs. The record is yet to be broken. Can you name this goalie?
Hint: His nickname was "Ulcers."

Frank McCool

20) In 1953–54, a Leafs goaltender recorded 13 shutouts, a mark that still stands as a club record. This goalie also won the Vezina Trophy that same year and was on a Stanley Cup-winning team with Detroit. Can you name him?

TORONTO
MAPLE
LEAFS
Bob Davidson

Flanked by teammates Howie Meeker and Sid Smith, captain Ted Kennedy leads a charge at the New York Rangers net.

21) The NHL's Hart Trophy winner in 1954 was a Chicago goaltender who had been traded to the Blackhawks by the Leafs a couple of years earlier. In fact, while with Toronto, this goalie played superbly in the 1951 finals when the Leafs won the Stanley Cup against Montreal. Who was he?

Leo Boivin, Tod Sloan, Jim Morrison and goalie Harry Lumley of the Leafs defend against Montreal's Maurice Richard.

22) This Maple Leafs right winger went on to be the first general manager for two NHL expansion teams. He first looked after the Philadelphia Flyers (1967) and then the Vancouver Canucks (1970). Who was he?

23) The Maple Leafs captain for the 1955–56 season was also the team's goal-scoring leader for four consecutive years, 1950–51 through 1954–55. He was also an NHL All-Star three times and played on three Stanley Cup-winning teams. Can you name him?

24) This left winger was the winner of several awards with the now-defunct New York Americans. As a member the Americans, he won the Calder Trophy in 1935 and the Art Ross in 1936 and 1937. He was also named to the NHL first (1935–36) and second (1936–37) All-Star Teams. As a Leaf, he continued his All-Star play by being named to the first team in 1940–41. He played on two Stanley Cup teams in Toronto (1942 and 1945) and is best remembered for scoring two goals in the seventh game of the 1942 finals against Detroit. Can you name him?

25) One of the two men the NHL has "suspended for life" was a former Maple Leafs right winger. He was actually the stick boy for the Leafs before he began his career as a player in 1939. He played on the great Leafs team of 1941–42 but was later traded to Detroit. He also played for Boston and New York. He was suspended in 1949 for gambling on hockey games. Can you name him?

26) During the late 1940s, two Maple Leafs defencemen became known as the "Gold Dust Twins." These two hard rocks were defensive stalwarts who helped the Leafs to four Stanley Cups, in 1947, 1948, 1949 and 1951. Can you name them?

Leafs defenceman Jim Thompson (#2) has Montreal's Jean Beliveau all wrapped up in front of the Toronto net.

27) Nicknamed "Sudden Death," this player scored three overtime winning goals in one playoff series with Boston (a 1939 semi-final against New York Rangers), establishing a record he shares with Maurice Richard. This player later went on to play for the Leafs and was on the Stanley Cup–winning team of 1944–45. Can you name him?

28) Do you know the nicknames of the following Maple Leafs players?
a) Harold Cotton
b) Rudolph Kampman
c) Wilfred McDonald
d) George Blair

29) Nicknamed "Wild Bill," this winger was known for his great desire to throw bodychecks despite his small stature. He was loved in Toronto but hated in opposing rinks. His aggressive style helped him to become the NHL penalty leader two years in a row while with the Leafs (1948–49 and 1949–50). He was also on three Maple Leafs Stanley Cup teams, but was eventually traded to Boston. Can you name him?

Leafs blueliner Fern Flaman tries to keep Boston's Leo Labine away from the Toronto net, guarded by Harry Lumley.

Toronto centre Tod Sloan (#15) tries to get one past New York goalie Johnny Bower.

30) Many Maple Leafs players have been successful in their careers off the ice. A right winger from Winnipeg who played with Toronto in the early 1940s was no exception—he became senior vice-president of International Nickel (INCO) after his hockey days were over. His hockey career was also successful: he was on teams that won the Allan Cup, the Memorial Cup and two Stanley Cups with the Leafs. The Allan Cup-winning team he was on was called the Trail Smoke Eaters—they went to Czechoslovakia in 1939 and won the world championship! Who was he?

31) This centre made the NHL second All-Star Team in 1955–56, the same year he led the Maple Leafs in goals scored and points. He may best be remembered for scoring the tying goal to send the fifth game of the 1951 finals into overtime with only 28 seconds to play. The Leafs scored in overtime to win the Stanley Cup. He played on two Toronto championship teams and was with the Chicago Blackhawks when they won the Cup in 1961. Who was he?

32) Two players from the 1951 Maple Leafs Stanley Cup–winning team were traded to the Boston Bruins, where they received All-Star recognition. One player, a centre, made the NHL second All-Star Team in 1954–55 and also led the league in penalty minutes that year. Can you name both these players?

33) Prior to Peter and Miroslav Ihnacak (1985–86), this set of brothers played together on the same Maple Leafs team in 1958–59. They each played their last game for Toronto that season. Can you name them?

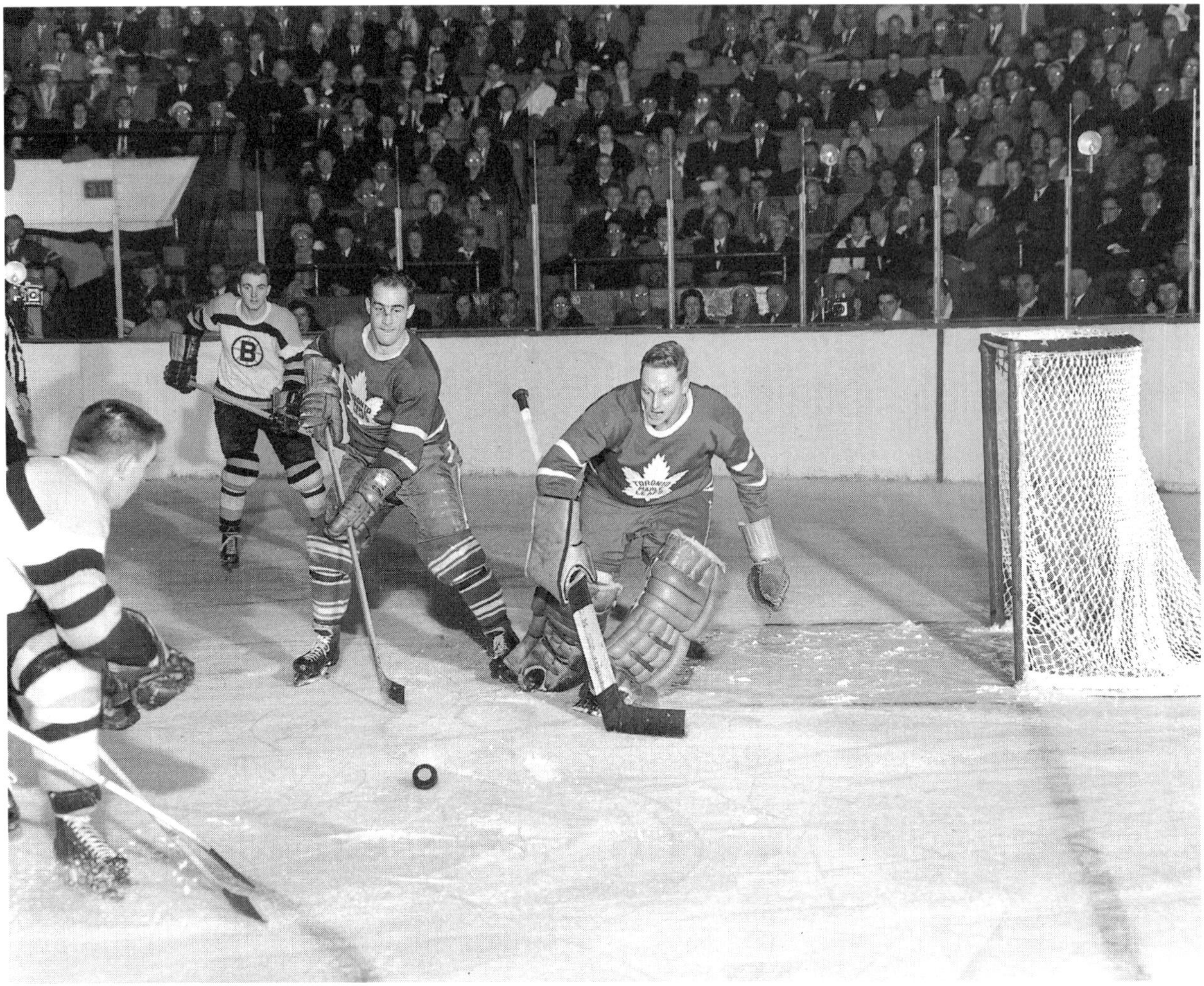

Leafs goaltender Ed Chadwick moves to clear the puck with the help of defenceman Jim Morrison.

34) In his first year with the Maple Leafs (1958–59), Johnny Bower was the backup for a goalie whom he would eventually replace as the Leafs' number-one netminder. Who was that goalie?

35) Only two men have been listed as the trainer on the Maple Leafs' 11 Stanley Cup teams. Can you name them?

36) One man looked after the equipment and skate sharpening for the Maple Leafs from the time the Gardens opened through to the 1980s, when he died. Who was he?

Brian Conacher (#22) helps to defend against the Red Wings.

37) During the early 1960s, Johnny Bower backstopped the Maple Leafs to three consecutive Stanley Cups. However, Bower was not in the net when the Leafs won their first Cup of the '60s in Chicago in April 1962. The goaltender who played in that game served as Bower's backup between 1961 and 1964. Can you name him?

38) Before the 1965–66 season, this Leaf surprised the hockey world by announcing his retirement. Then, during the 1979–80 season, he shocked the hockey world by coming out of retirement to attempt a comeback with Toronto. Can you name this unpredictable Leaf?

39) The leading scorer in the 1967 playoffs also scored the Stanley Cup–winning goal for the Leafs in the sixth game of the finals versus Montreal. Despite these achievements he would be traded away in 1968. Can you name him?

40) During the 1967 Stanley Cup playoffs, a young Leafs winger made a somewhat unexpected contribution. A former member of the Canadian National Team, he scored the winning goal in the last game of the semifinals against Chicago. He also scored the winning goal in the crucial fifth game against Montreal in the finals. However, in June 1968 the Leafs left him unprotected in the draft,

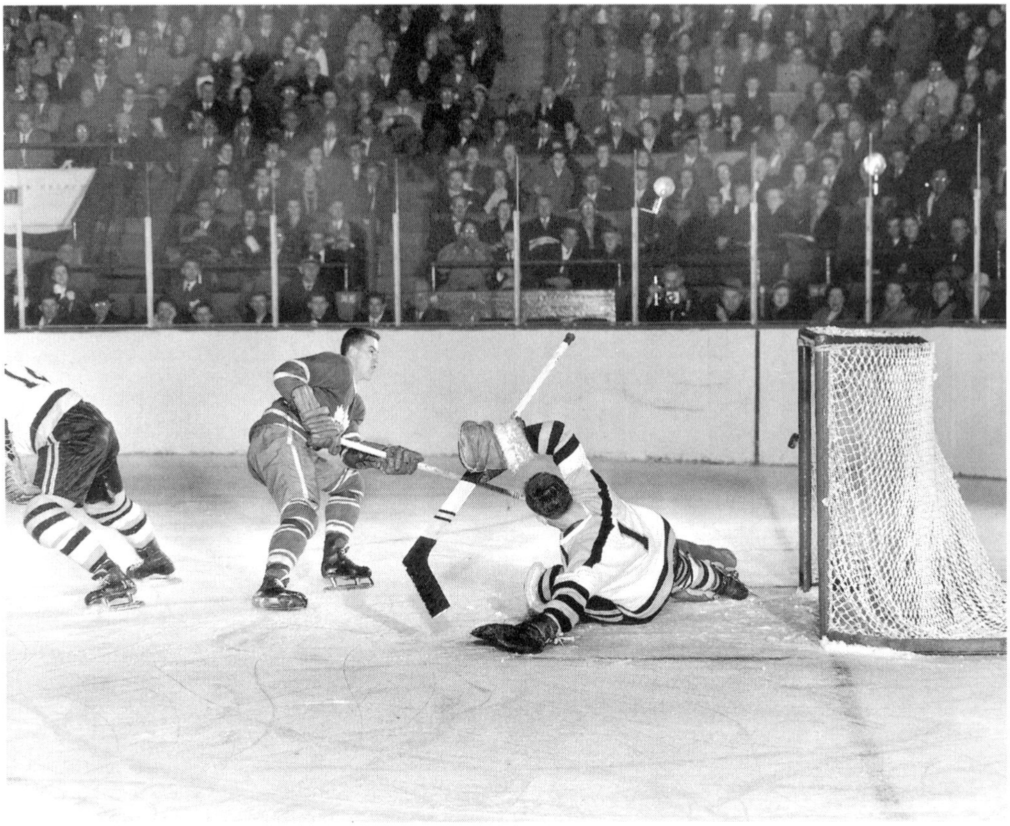

Billy Harris scores on Boston's Terry Sawchuk.

and he was taken by Detroit, where he finished his NHL career. Can you name him? *Hint: His family name is well known in hockey circles and Canadian athletics in general. In fact, his father Lionel was named Canada's Athlete of the Half Century.*

41) In the 1970–71 season, the Maple Leafs had a rookie right winger who was a native of Prince Edward Island. After spending several seasons with the Canadian National Team, he came to the Leafs and scored 22 goals in his first season. However, the next year he scored only 10 goals and was later lost in the expansion draft to the Atlanta Flames. Can you name him? *Hint: He went on to be an assistant coach with the New York Islanders during their Stanley Cup-winning season of 1979–80. He later became head coach of the Colorado Rockies/New Jersey Devils.*

42) A former great Leafs All-Star defenceman and long-time club executive had a son who played parts of three different seasons with Toronto during the late 1960s and early 1970s. Although the son played the same position as his father, that is where the resemblance ended. He played in 86 games with Toronto, scoring six goals and a grand total of 12 points. He also played for the Oakland Seals. Can you name the player who never matched

the ability of his famous and colourful dad?

Jim McKenny and Jim Dorey (#8) watch Chicago's Eric Nesterenko.

43) This former Leaf who played with Toronto from 1955 to 1965 was best known as a utility forward—a pinch hitter when injuries struck. He ended up on three Stanley Cup-winning teams with Toronto and went on to play for the Detroit Red Wings, the Oakland Seals and the Pittsburgh Penguins. After his playing days were over, he was better known as the coach of the Toronto Toros, the Swedish and Italian national teams, the Hamilton "Junior A" Red Wings and Team Canada 1974 (WHA edition). Can you name him?

44) Prior to the Maple Leafs' three consecutive Stanley Cup victories between 1962 and 1964, the Chicago Blackhawks won the championship in 1961. One player was a member of all four teams. Can you name the player who sipped champagne from the Stanley Cup four consecutive years?

45) One of the very few people to wear glasses while playing in the NHL was a former Leafs defenceman. He was a member of two Stanley Cup–winning teams: Toronto in the early 1960s, and the Detroit Red Wings Stanley Cup team of 1954. He also played for the St. Louis Blues, a team he later coached. However, his greatest success as a coach came with another NHL team—the New York Islanders. Can you name him?

46) The second player ever to win the Bill Masterson Memorial Trophy (given to the NHL player who best exemplifies the qualities of perseverance, sportsmanship and dedication to hockey) was a former Leaf who started his NHL career with Toronto during the 1959–60 season. He also played for the New York Rangers, Detroit Red Wings, Oakland Seals and Minnesota North Stars before going to the WHA. Can you name him?

47) In his first game at Maple Leaf Gardens, this former Leafs defenceman set an NHL record (since broken) when he received four minor penalties, two majors, two 10-minute misconducts, and one game misconduct on October 16, 1968, against the Pittsburgh

Penguins. He would be traded by the Leafs to the New York Rangers in 1972 but would play again in Toronto as a member of the WHA Toros. His style of play made him popular with the fans. Can you name him and the player the Leafs received in exchange when he was traded?
Hint: The player the Leafs acquired in the trade with New York would play only one full season in Toronto before going on to play in Detroit and Minnesota.

48) The first general manager of the Los Angeles Kings (who later became their coach) was a former Toronto Maple Leaf. He started his career with the Boston Bruins and won the Calder Trophy as the best rookie in 1957. The Leafs acquired him in 1958, and he was instrumental in Toronto's playoff drives in the late 1950s through to 1961. Can you name him?

49) This Toronto scout was largely responsible for the Leafs' signing then unknown Swedes Inge Hammarstrom and Borje Salming in 1973. These were important signings because the NHL found a new source of talent in Europe. The scout in question played at one time for the Leafs and saw action as a goaltender during the 1960–61 and 1969–70 seasons. He later became the Leafs' general manager. Can you name him?

50) This much-travelled goalie started his career with Toronto before going on to play for the Montreal Canadiens, New York Rangers, Minnesota North Stars and Vancouver Canucks. However, he might be best known for giving up goals of historical significance. For example, while in the net for the Leafs on March 16, 1961, he gave up Bernie Geoffrion's 50th goal. That goal meant Geoffrion became the first player to score 50 since Rocket Richard had done so. Also, as a member of the New York Rangers in 1965, this goalie allowed Bobby Hull's 51st goal of the season. That goal made Hull the first man to score more than 50 goals in one season—quite an accomplishment back then! Can you name this goaltender?

Garry Monahan

Rene Robert (#14) and Darryl Sittler (#27) attack the Pittsburgh net.

51) The first coach and general manager of the Oakland Seals was a former Maple Leaf who was an important member of the 1962 Stanley Cup team. Known for his hard-nosed style both on and off the ice, he was acquired by the Leafs from Montreal, where he had been a member of four Stanley Cup–winning teams during the 1950s. Can you name him? *Hint: Until Darryl Sittler had his 10-point night in 1976, this player shared the NHL record with Rocket Richard for most points in one game—eight (four goals and four assists on January 9, 1954 when Montreal defeated Chicago 12–1).*

Toronto forwards (l to r) Billy Harris, Bob Pulford and Ron Stewart look for the loose puck against goalie Glenn Hall of Chicago.

52) While playing Junior A hockey with the Toronto Marlboros, this defenceman was often compared to Bobby Orr. Although he did not live up to this advance billing, his slick stickhandling did enable him to score 327 points with the Leafs during his eight seasons with Toronto, where he split his playing time between defence and right wing. He ended up being sold to the Minnesota North Stars before leaving hockey. In addition to his quick wit, he was known for doing on-the-ice scenes for actor Art Hindle in the hockey movie *Face-Off*. He later became a sportscaster in Toronto. Can you name him?

53) After playing with the Minnesota North Stars, California Golden Seals, Boston Bruins, Detroit Red Wings, Washington Capitals and Cleveland Barons, the Maple Leafs' number-one draft choice of 1963 finally put on a Toronto uniform for the first time in the 1978–79 season. Despite scoring

25 goals that year, he was subsequently traded away the next season to the Colorado Rockies. Can you name this well-travelled centreman?

54) The Montreal Canadiens' first-round selection and the first player chosen overall in the 1963 amateur draft eventually had two stints with the Toronto Maple Leafs. The Leafs first acquired him from Los Angeles when they dealt a long-time veteran to get this left winger. The Leafs then traded him to Vancouver in a deal that brought Dave Dunn to Toronto at the start of the 1974–75 season. Toronto re-acquired him from the Canucks for the 1978–79 season, which was to be his last in the NHL. Can you name him?

55) Before becoming a defenceman for the Maple Leafs, this player delivered milk in

Larry Hillman (#22) and Terry Sawchuk keep an eye on Montreal's John Ferguson.

Orillia, Ontario, where he played for the Orillia Terriers. He became known as "The Milkman" and he played parts of three seasons with Toronto before he was sold to the Vancouver Canucks. Can you name him?

56) After being a member of the 1974 Stanley Cup–champion Philadelphia Flyers, this left winger was acquired by the Leafs in the hopes that he could fill one of their vital needs. However, the man nicknamed "Cowboy," who had once scored 43 goals in one season, lasted only one year in Toronto, recording 15 goals. He was claimed by Atlanta on waivers and played there for a year and a half before moving to the Edmonton Oilers of the WHA. Can you name him?
Hint: He was very noticeable on the ice because of his beard.

57) The first-ever captain of the Vancouver Canucks was a former Maple Leaf who played one season (1965–66) in Toronto. He also played for the New York Rangers and the Boston Bruins. Can you name him?
Hint: He was well known for his fighting ability. He went on to coach the Canucks for a season and a half.

Pat Quinn checks Boston's Bobby Orr (#4) in front of the Maple Leafs net.

58) The Buffalo Sabres started their hockey operations in the 1970–71 season. Their first captain was a former Leaf. Toronto had acquired him from Detroit, and he had played previously with the New York Rangers and the Boston Bruins before finishing his career in Buffalo. Can you name him?
Hint: He went on to coach the Sabres, taking them to the finals in 1975, and he later coached the Leafs.

59) A member of the Boston Bruins, "Uke Line" once played for the Maple Leafs. He tied Bobby Hull for the NHL goal-scoring lead in the 1959–60 season (39 goals). His stay with the Leafs during the 1962–63 season was brief. Other stops for this centreman included the New York Rangers, Montreal Canadiens, Chicago Blackhawks and Minnesota North Stars. Can you name him?

60) After starting his career in Toronto (his last year with the Leafs was 1959–60), this defenceman went on to play for Montreal, Chicago, the New York Rangers and the Pittsburgh Penguins. He coached the Montreal Canadiens to a stunning Stanley Cup victory in 1971. He was nonetheless replaced the following year. He then went on to coach the Atlanta Flames. Can you name him?
Hint: While this former Leaf was coaching Montreal to the Stanley Cup win, Henri Richard called him "the worst coach [he had] ever played for."

61) When Bernie Parent left the Leafs to go to the WHA at the start of the 1972–73 season, the team was left with only one veteran goaltender—Jacques Plante. The situation forced the Leafs to let a 1970 eighth-round draft choice assume the bulk of the goaltending duties during that year. Can you name the goalie?
Hint: The goaltender went on to play for Washington, Detroit, Quebec, Edmonton and New Jersey.

62) Johnny Bower's career was, for all practical purposes, over in 1969–70. In fact, he only played one game that season. That left the goaltending chores to Bruce Gamble and another veteran puck-stopper. This

Don Marshall

goaltender played in 25 games that year, recording one shutout, but was gone by the next season. Can you name the Leafs' backup goaltender for the 1969–70 season?
Hint: He started his NHL career with Pittsburgh and ended it with the Oakland Seals.

Goaltender Gord McRae goes behind the net to clear a puck.

63) After starting his career with the Maple Leafs in 1970–71, this right winger played in Pittsburgh before achieving some measure of stardom with the Buffalo Sabres. It was in Buffalo that he enjoyed his greatest years as a member of the "French Connection" line, earning a second-team All-Star berth in 1974–75. Can you name him?
Hint: He scored three overtime goals for Buffalo in playoff action, including one memorable goal in the fog against Philadelphia's Bernie Parent in the 1975 finals. He was traded by Buffalo to Colorado, and was re-acquired by the Leafs in the 1980–81 season.

Goalie Jacques Plante (#1) and defenceman Mike Pelyk (#4) defend against Stan Mikita of Chicago.

64) This former Leafs right winger played a total of 21 NHL seasons, appearing in more than 1,300 games and scoring 278 career goals. He won three consecutive Stanley Cup championships with the Leafs from 1962 to 1964, but was traded by Toronto to Boston in 1965. He went on to play for St. Louis, the New York

Rangers, the Vancouver Canucks and the New York Islanders. He then went into the coaching field, handling the New York Rangers briefly in 1975–76 and the Los Angeles Kings for the entire 1977–78 season. Can you name him?

65) This Leafs defenceman was a member of all four Maple Leafs Stanley Cup–winning teams during the 1960s but he was also a much-travelled player. In his 12 NHL seasons, in addition to playing for the Leafs, he played for Detroit, Boston, Minnesota, Montreal, Philadelphia, Los Angeles and Buffalo. He was on Stanley Cup–winning teams with Detroit and Montreal, making him a member of six championship teams—not a bad record for a player who was essentially a fifth defenceman. Can you name him? *Hint: He had a brother who played in the NHL at the same time he did.*

66) This centreman started his NHL career with the Maple Leafs in 1968–69 after a junior career with the Toronto Marlboros, but his time with the Leafs was shortlived and he was traded to Philadelphia that same year. Buffalo drafted this player from the Flyers, and he later became the Sabres' captain. Never a prolific goal scorer, he did score one goal of particular significance. On the final night of the 1971–72 season, this player scored with just four seconds left to play, giving Buffalo a tie against Philadelphia, which knocked the Flyers out of a playoff position and allowed Pittsburgh to go into post-season action. He also played with Vancouver, Atlanta and Washington. Can you name him?

67) This former NHL defenceman started playing with the Leafs during the 1968–69 season, when the team was going with youth behind the blueline. Although his stay in Toronto lasted only two years, he is perhaps best remembered for a devastating check he delivered to superstar Bobby Orr during the 1969 playoffs. The check knocked Orr unconscious, and outraged Boston fans tried to get at the Leafs defenceman in the penalty box, forcing him to flee. He moved on to play for Vancouver, and later to the Atlanta Flames where he was captain for two years. After his playing days were over, he moved into coaching, leading the Philadelphia Flyers (in 1980) and later the Vancouver Canucks (in 1994) to Stanley Cup final appearances. Can you name him?

68) This former NHL "iron man" who played in 580 consecutive games was with the Leafs during the 1959–60 and 1960–61 seasons, during which he kept his streak intact. He had previously played with Detroit and Chicago, and after his stay with Toronto, he was a New York Ranger. He started his coaching career with Los Angeles before going on to coach Detroit, Colorado and Pittsburgh. Can you name him? *Hint: He was named coach of Team Canada in the 1977 World Cup Tournament in Vienna.*

69) The Maple Leafs drafted this winger from Buffalo for the 1971–72 season, hoping the experienced veteran could help the team as he had Buffalo the previous year in scoring 20 goals for the expansion Sabres. Despite the fact that he had more than 250 career goals, his best years were behind him by the time he played for Toronto. He was a disappointment

in Toronto, scoring only two goals in 50 games. He had been a member of the Montreal Canadiens teams that won five consecutive Stanley Cups (1956 to 1960) before being traded to the New York Rangers in 1963. He stayed with New York until 1970, when Punch Imlach, then with Buffalo, convinced him to play with the Sabres. After retirement he became a colour commentator on *Hockey Night in Canada* for the Montreal telecasts. Can you name him?

70) This former Leafs goaltender was particularly known for his wandering ways. He wandered through many NHL teams, including Toronto, Oakland, Chicago, Vancouver, Washington and Minnesota. During play, he was known to rush out to the centre redline stickhandling with the puck. In 1971–72 while with Chicago, he stayed still long enough to share in the winning of the Vezina Trophy. Can you name him?

Jimmy Jones

71) During the 1978–79 season, this former Leafs centre scored only seven goals during the regular season, but during the preliminary round playoff series against the Los Angeles Kings he tied an NHL goal-scoring playoff record. It was in the first game of the best-of-three series that this player scored three goals in one period to tie the NHL playoff record. Can you name him?
Hint: He was a former first-round draft choice taken from the Toronto Marlboros in 1972.

72) The Maple Leafs have not had anyone on their team win the Art Ross Trophy (given to the leading point scorer during the season) since 1938. However, they did have a former two-time Art Ross winner play for them during the 1964–65 season. He was the goal-scoring champion for the 1957–58 season and played on five consecutive Stanley Cup–winning teams with Montreal during the mid- and late 1950s. He also scored the Stanley Cup–winning goal for Montreal in 1957 against Boston. He had more than 260 career goals, but during his brief stay in Toronto, he scored only two goals in 38 games. He finished his career with the St. Louis Blues. Can you name him?

73) This former Leafs defenceman was one of only two Toronto players to win the Hart Trophy as the NHL's most valuable player. He went on to help build the Vancouver Canucks franchise. Later, this Hall of Fame member became a *Hockey Night in Canada* broadcaster, mostly for games played from Vancouver. His son played for the Maple Leafs at the end of the 1976–77 season when Toronto needed help along the blueline. The son was acquired from Colorado, but he had NHL experience in Oakland, Pittsburgh, Buffalo and Vancouver. The time he spent with the Leafs would end his NHL career. Who was he and who was his famous dad?

74) In the 1974–75 season, the Los Angeles Kings accumulated 105 points while the Leafs managed only 78. Yet when the two teams met in the best-of-three preliminary round playoff series, the Leafs won 2 games to 1. In that series, the Leafs had to rely on the goal-tending of a little-known minor leaguer summoned from Oklahoma City. That upset of the Kings was to be his only NHL highlight. He stayed with Toronto through the 1977–78 season, during which he was used primarily as the backup goalie, before he retired from hockey. Can you name him?

The Canadiens' Jacques Plante covers up the puck against the Leafs' Eric Nesterenko (#16).

75) In 1976 the Leafs made defenceman Randy Carlyle their number-one draft choice. However, the Leafs almost lost Carlyle to Cincinnati of the WHA, who claimed they had Carlyle's signature on a contract. It turned out that Carlyle had only signed a letter of intent. After some controversy, Cincinnati finally waived all rights to Carlyle when the Leafs agreed to assume the contract of another defenceman. Can you name this other player?
Hint: He was a former Leaf who had left the team to jump to the WHA in 1974. He was also a member of the Memorial Cup–winning Toronto Marlboros of 1967.

76) In June 1975, the Leafs sent their number-one draft choice for 1976 to the Montreal Canadiens for a goaltender who had not played a single moment in the 1974–75 season. However, he saw plenty of action with the Leafs in 1975–76, playing in 64 games with a 3.19 goals-against average. One year later he played in only 33 games, losing his job to Mike Palmateer. In October 1977 the New York Rangers claimed him from Toronto in the league waiver draft. Can you name this goaltender?
Hint: He won the Molson Cup in Montreal for the 1973–74 season when he took on the bulk of the team's goaltending duties in place of the then-retired Ken Dryden.

77) The New York Islanders picked centre Bryan Trottier in the 1974 amateur draft as an underage selection. Trottier was the Islanders' second choice in the 1974 draft and was picked 22nd overall. Trottier would become the key man down the middle when the Islanders won the Stanley Cup four years in a row. In that same draft, the Leafs used their first pick, 13th overall, to take a centre who, like Trottier, was an underage junior at the time. Trottier decided to play junior hockey for one more year despite being drafted, while the Leafs selection decided to turn pro immediately. Can you name the player the Leafs picked?
Hint: He was traded away by the Leafs by the start of the 1978–79 season.

78) The Winnipeg Jets had a horrendous season in 1980–81. They lost 57 games that year and went an NHL-record 30 games without a victory. The Jets fired head coach Tom McVie in mid-season and replaced him with a man who had played with the Leafs during the 1968–69 season. Can you name him?
Hint: He also played for St. Louis, Philadelphia, Detroit and Montreal.

79) This former Leafs centre went wild during a playoff game versus the Boston Bruins on April 2, 1969, and set many NHL and Leafs team records. His marks include most penalties in one playoff game (eight, since tied) and most penalty minutes in one period (34, since surpassed by Dave Schultz). He capped his evening of madness by punching a linesman, which led to his suspension for the balance of the playoffs. His exuberance did not help the Leafs that night: they lost 10–0, and eventually lost the series in four straight games. Can you name the penalty record setter?
Hint: The Leafs had acquired him from Philadelphia. He also played for Chicago, Detroit and Boston during his career.

80) The last man to score six goals in one game prior to Darryl Sittler was Red Berenson, who did it on November 8, 1968, when the St. Louis Blues whipped Philadelphia 8–0. The goaltender, who allowed all six of Berenson's goals that night, went on to play for the Leafs during the 1970s. Can you name him?

Leafs goaltender Ken Wregget (#31) gets help from Luke Richardson (#2) in front of the goal.

81) The Boston Bruins made this former Peterborough Petes centre their second-round draft choice (31st overall) in 1973. However, he never had a chance to play in the NHL until the Leafs signed him as a free agent in 1977. He played two years in Toronto, mostly as a penalty killer and on the checking line. At the age of 28 he would end his playing career and try his hand at coaching junior hockey with the Toronto Marlboros. Can you name him?

82) The assistant general manager/director of scouting for the New York Islanders for the 1984–85 season was a former Maple Leaf who was a member of the 1963–64 Stanley Cup team. He was often called up from the minors around playoff time and would often score key goals. His NHL career included stops in Boston, Detroit and Oakland. Can you name him?

83) Although he started his career with the Maple Leafs in 1952–53, this left winger had his greatest success with the Detroit Red Wings. In fact, he played on a line with two Red Wing legends, Gordie Howe and Alex Delvecchio. His NHL career also took him to the New York Rangers and the Minnesota North Stars. When his playing career was over, he coached the North Stars (1973–74) and the Los Angeles Kings (1981–82). Who was he?

84) This big right winger was a member of the Chicago Blackhawks Stanley Cup team of 1961. He ended up playing more than 1,000 games for Chicago over 16 seasons. He scored 200 goals for Chicago, and his aggressive play helped him to accumulate more than 1,000 career penalty minutes. He started his career with the Maple Leafs in 1951–52 and stayed with Toronto until 1956. He was the Leafs' third leading scorer in 1954–55. Can you name him?

85) Two players listed on the Maple Leafs' Stanley Cup team roster of 1967 never played a game during the regular season (1966–67). Since they did play for Toronto during the 1967 playoffs, their names are on the Stanley Cup. Can you name these two players with excellent timing?

86) Three former Leafs defencemen have coached the St. Louis Blues since that franchise began operations in 1967. Al Arbour is one of the players in question. Who are the other two?

87) In the 1978 entry draft, the Leafs made defenceman Joel Quenneville their first selection, 21st overall (in the second round). The Leafs had received the choice as compensation for the St. Louis Blues' signing of another Leafs defenceman. Who was the player the Blues signed?
Hint: This player was Toronto property twice during his NHL career and had a brother who played for the Buffalo Sabres.

88) In the 1979 entry draft, the Leafs selected a promising goaltender from the Quebec Remparts with their third choice. His first chance at a heavy workload came in 1981–82, when he played in 40 games and looked like the goalie of the future. However, he played only one game for the Leafs the following year, and one year after that he was traded to Pittsburgh. Who was he?

89) In 1980–81, the Leafs featured a Czechoslovakian goaltender and a Czech defenceman. Both played in more than 50 games that year. Both had also played for the Czech national team, and within two years both were dropped by the Leafs. Can you name them?

Mike Foligno

90) In the 1979 entry draft, the Maple Leafs' second choice was a centre from the Sherbrooke Beavers who had scored 91 goals in his final junior year. On a team that needed a big goal scorer at centre, his future looked promising. He did score 14 goals in his first 43 games with Toronto in 1981–82, but this turned out to be the high point of his career with the Leafs. He was released two years later. Who was he?

91) With their fourth choice in the 1977 entry draft, the Leafs took a small right winger from the Lethbridge Broncos. He made it to the Leafs during the 1978–79 season, when he played in 16 games. He had started that year in the minors with New Brunswick (AHL) and was named the league's most valuable player, leading the league in goal

scoring. He was not as successful with the Leafs and was dealt away to Pittsburgh by 1983. Who was he?

92) For the start of the 1984–85 season, the New Jersey Devils selected a new coach who had previously been in the Maple Leafs organization. He had been coaching the Leafs' minor league team in St. Catharines, and prior to that had coached the Cornwall Royals to the Memorial Cup in 1980. In 1985, he coached Team Canada to the silver medal in the World Championships—Canada's best showing in years. Can you name him? *Hint: He coached the Leafs in 1989–90 to a 38–38–2 record.*

93) To start the 1984–85 season, the Maple Leafs decided to go with two youngsters in net. One was drafted in the fourth round in 1982 and the other was Toronto's third pick in 1983. Both ended up in the minors by the end of the season. Who are the two goalies in question?

94) This right winger was Detroit's first-round draft choice (11th overall) in 1980 and went on to play for the New York Rangers and the Pittsburgh Penguins. He was signed by Toronto as a free agent in 1987 and played in 27 games with the Leafs, scoring four goals between 1987 and 1988. Can you name him?

95) In 1986, the Montreal Canadiens won the Stanley Cup by defeating the Calgary Flames in five games. It marked the first time since 1967 that two Canadian teams met for the Stanley Cup. Two members of the Montreal team were at one time players with the Maple Leafs. One was a defenceman and the other was a right winger. Can you name both?

96) With their first draft pick in 1980, the Leafs took a defenceman (25th overall). He ended up playing only 19 regular-season games with Toronto before the Edmonton Oilers signed him as a free agent in 1986. He later played on two Stanley Cup–winning teams with the Oilers. Who is he?

97) For the first time in their history, the Leafs used their 1986 first-round draft selection to take a French-Canadian hockey player who had an outstanding final junior year with the Laval Titans. Who is he?

98) In one of the worst moves the Leafs ever made, a certain restricted free agent was signed from the Dallas Stars in July 1994. The Stars took the matter to arbitration to settle the compensation issue, but Toronto's offer of Peter Zezel and Grant Marshall was accepted by the arbitrator (the Stars wanted Kenny Jonsson). Who was the big bust Toronto signed?

99) A former captain of the Montreal Canadiens (and a member of the 1993 Stanley Cup–winning team for the Habs), this centre was acquired by the Leafs from the New York Islanders in a trade involving goalie Damien Rhodes. The centre's arrival in Toronto was very much anticipated, but his stay proved to be brief and he was dealt to Florida for a young prospect. Name the player and the prospect the Leafs got from the Panthers in exchange.

100) Picked up on waivers from the New York Islanders, this winger was teamed with Peter Zezel and Mark Osborne to form a very effective checking line in 1992–93 and 1993–94. Can you name him?

101) A former 50-goal scorer for the Pittsburgh Penguins, this centre was picked up by the Leafs in a deal with Philadelphia (for future considerations) in 1991 to give the team some much-needed offence. He would play only one year as a Leaf (with 14 goals) before being let go. Can you name him?
Hint: He also played for the Calgary Flames and was speared in a playoff game by Marty McSorley of the Edmonton Oilers.

Defenceman Brad Marsh (#3) covers up in front of goalie Allan Bester.

102) Originally drafted by Boston, this player was dealt to Edmonton, where he shared in four Oilers Stanley Cup victories. He was later moved to Los Angeles in the famous deal involving Wayne Gretzky, and the Leafs got him in a trade for John McIntyre. Can you name him?

103) A former captain of the Buffalo Sabres, this right winger was acquired by the Leafs in a trade involving Brian Curran and the popular Lou Franceschetti. In addition to his good play, this player was well known for his leap after scoring a goal. Can you name him?

104) As a long-time member of the Washington Capitals, this centre produced good numbers before the Leafs picked him up in a June 1994 deal for Rob Pearson. He lasted one year in Toronto (the shortened 1994–95 season) and was dealt to Vancouver for the lamentable Sergio Momesso. Can you name the player?

105) After a long career with the New York Islanders, this native of Hamilton, Ontario, was signed as a free agent by the Leafs in July 1997. He scored 45 goals for Toronto, but his very poor play in the 1999 playoffs sealed his fate as a Maple Leaf and a deal was struck with St. Louis. Can you name the player?
Hint: He scored the last-ever Toronto goal at Maple Leaf Gardens.

106) The first selection made by Cliff Fletcher in an entry draft for the Leafs was a righthanded shooting centre from the Belleville Bulls who was chosen in 1992. Although he had good speed and some offensive skill, he was not a favourite of then Leafs coach Pat Burns. Eventually he was dealt to Vancouver in exchange for Lonny Bohonos. Can you name him?

107) Although he played only two full seasons as a Maple Leaf, this former Calgary Flame and Philadelphia Flyer was a very popular member of the team between 1988 (when he was picked up in the waiver draft) and 1991. He would skate around the centre-ice circle at Maple Leaf Gardens when he was selected as one of the three stars and the crowd would roar its approval. Never a great skater, this blueliner always gave it his all and finished his playing days with the Ottawa Senators in the 1992–93 season. Can you name him?

George Hainsworth was the Leafs' goalie between 1933 and 1937.

108) This defenceman, who had played with the Detroit Red Wings when they won the Stanley Cup in 1998, was signed as a free agent in July of 2001. He did not work out so well for the Maple Leafs and spent most of his time in the minors with the Leafs' farm club in St. John's. Name him.

109) When the Boston Bruins lost a contract arbitration decision to a player who was skilled but a less-than-stellar playoff performer, they quickly moved to dump him and his new deal. The found a willing buyer in the Maple Leafs, but this right winger only scored 15 goals and 39 points in 80 games for Toronto before he was dealt off to Washington. Name him.

110) As a member of the 1994 Stanley Cup champion New York Rangers team, this netminder was signed as a free agent by the Leafs to back up starter Felix Potvin in 1997. He stayed in that role even when the team signed Curtis Joseph, but he only played 68 games as a Leaf (posting a mediocre 23–30–5 record) before he was let go prior to the start of the 2001–02 season. Name him.

111) After the 2000–01 season, this goaltender was looking for work when the Maple Leafs called and invited him to their training camp. He made the team and filled in admirably when Curtis Joseph was injured (posting a very respectable 12–10–5 record), but Toronto failed to re-sign him for the 2002–03 season. Instead he went back to his original NHL team, the New Jersey Devils. Name him. *Hint: He also played for Tampa Bay and Vancouver.*

112) Drafted 15th overall by the Maple Leafs in 1995 (bypassing such players as Petr Sykora, Denis Gauthier and Martin Biron), this large defenceman played only 15 games as a Leaf (no goals, no assists and six penalty minutes) before he was traded to Florida in February of 1999. Name him.

113) Originally drafted by the Maple Leafs in 1991 (47th overall), this gifted goal scorer spent three seasons with the farm team in St. John's (scoring 132 goals in 203 games) but never got much of a chance with the big club (playing in only 13 games). He was dealt to Los Angeles but the Leafs re-acquired him in March of 1999, and he enjoyed a 24-goal season with the team in the 2000–01 campaign. He was let go as a free agent and he signed with the Montreal Canadiens. Name him.

114) One of the few players in Leafs history to score his first goal with the team in the playoffs (in 2000 against New Jersey), this small but speedy left winger was selected 57th overall by Toronto in the 1997 entry draft. He was traded to Vancouver for former first-round Canucks draft choice Josh Holden (12th overall in 1996). Can you name the player the Leafs selected out of Boston College?

115) Drafted 40th overall by Vancouver in 1995, this hulking (6'8", 240 pounds) defenceman was acquired by the Leafs in a deal that sent Darby Hendrickson to the Canucks in exchange. The blueliner made quite an impression when he pounded out a clear victory in a fight with Rich Pilon of the New York Islanders, but did nothing else.

Jim Dorey (#8) takes out Bob Pulford of the Los Angeles Kings along the boards.

Toronto dealt the defenceman to Philadelphia, who later moved him to Colorado. Can you name him?

116) Acquired in a deal with New Jersey, this aggressive defenceman excelled under coach Mike Murphy but fell into disfavour when Pat Quinn took over the Leafs. Associate general manager Mike Smith made a terrible deal by sending the blossoming blueliner to Edmonton for nothing more than second-round and fourth-round draft choices (Jonathan Zion and Kris Vernarsky, neither of whom remain with the organization). He found his game as an Oiler and was even named captain, while the Leafs are still looking for a defenceman who plays his type of game! Name him.

Answers

1) Carl Voss
2) Red Horner
3) Lorne Chabot
4) George Hainsworth
5) Syd Howe
6) Frank Nighbor
7) George Parsons
8) Frank Selke
9) William "Flash" Hollett
10) Alf Moore
11) Lorne Carr
12) Baz Bastien
13) Paul Bibeault
14) Joe Primeau

Goalie Wayne Thomas (#30) was acquired in a deal with Montreal.

15) Syl Apps, Sr.
16) Gus Bodnar
17) Bob Davidson
18) Nick and Don Metz
19) Frank McCool
20) Harry Lumley
21) Al Rollins
22) Norman "Bud" Poile
23) Sid Smith
24) Dave "Sweeney" Schriner
25) Billy Taylor
26) Gus Mortson and Jim Thomson
27) Mel Hill
28) a) "Baldy"
    b) "Bingo"
    c) "Bucko"
    d) "Dusty"
29) Bill Ezinicki
30) John McCreedy
31) Tod Sloan
32) Fleming Mackell and Fern Flaman
33) Brian and Barry Cullen
34) Ed Chadwick
35) Tim Daly (seven Cup teams): Bob Haggert (four Cup teams)
36) Tommy Naylor
37) Don Simmons
38) Carl Brewer
39) Jim Pappin
40) Brian Conacher
41) Billy MacMillan
42) Terry Clancy, son of King Clancy
43) Billy Harris
44) Ed Litzenberger
45) Al Arbour coached the New York Islanders to four consecutive Stanley Cups.
46) Ted Hampson, who won the Masterton in 1969.
47) The defenceman was Jim Dorey, and he was traded by the Leafs to the Rangers for Pierre Jarry.
48) Larry Regan
49) Gerry McNamara
50) Cesare Maniago
51) Bert Olmstead
52) Jim McKenny

JACK VALIQUETTE

Doug Favell was picked up in a trade with Philadelphia.

Forward Bill Berg (#10) knew how to make himself unpopular with the opposition.

53) Walt McKechnie
54) Garry Monahan
55) Claire Alexander
56) Bill Flett
57) Orland Kurtenbach
58) Floyd Smith
59) Bronco Horvath
60) Al MacNeil
61) Ron Low
62) Marv Edwards
63) Rene Robert
64) Ron Stewart
65) Larry Hillman
66) Gerry Meehan
67) Pat Quinn
68) Johnny Wilson
69) Don Marshall
70) Gary Smith
71) George Ferguson (Tim Kerr and Mario Lemieux now share the record of four)
72) Dickie Moore
73) Tracy Pratt (son) and Walter "Babe" Pratt (father)
74) Gord McRae
75) Mike Pelyk
76) Wayne Thomas
77) Jack Valiquette
78) Bill Sutherland
79) Forbes Kennedy
80) Doug Favell
81) Jimmy Jones
82) Gerry Ehman
83) Parker MacDonald
84) Eric Nesterenko
85) Milan Marcetta and Autry Erickson
86) Leo Boivin and Joel Quenneville
87) Rod Seiling
88) Vince Tremblay
89) The goaltender was Jiri Crha and the defenceman was Vitezslav Duris.
90) Norman Aubin
91) Rocky Saganiuk
92) Doug Carpenter
93) Ken Wregget and Allan Bester

Vincent Damphousse (#10) battles in front of the New Jersey net.

94) Mike Blaisdell
95) Gaston Gingras and Alain Belanger
96) Craig Muni
97) Vincent Damphousse
98) Mike Craig
99) Kirk Muller was traded to Florida for Jason Podollan.
100) Bill Berg
101) Mike Bullard
102) Mike Krushelnyski
103) Mike Foligno
104) Mike Ridley
105) Derek King
106) Brandon Convery
107) Brad Marsh
108) Anders Eriksson
109) Dmitri Khristich
110) Glenn Healy
111) Corey Schwab
112) Jeff Ware
113) Yanic Perreault
114) Jeff Farkas
115) Chris McAllister
116) Jason Smith

Mike Krushelnyski

Ron Stewart (#12) has to contend with Montreal's Doug Harvey (#2) and goalie Jacques Plante (#1).

5

Did You Know?

1) Toronto's NHL franchise was officially recognized with the nickname "Maple Leafs" on February 14, 1927. Prior to that, the franchise had had two other nicknames. What were they?
Hint: Both teams won the Stanley Cup.

2) Only one man has both coached and captained a Toronto Maple Leafs team to victory in the Stanley Cup. Who is he?

The Leafs have just won the 1947 Stanley Cup against the Montreal Canadiens.

3) The most famous line the Leafs ever had was known as the "Kid Line." This trio terrorized the NHL during the 1930s. Which players made up the line?

4) After the Leafs won their first Stanley Cup in 1931–32, they made the finals another six times in the years to 1940 and lost each time. Can you name the teams the Leafs lost the Cup to in those six years?

5) Who were the general manager and coach of the Leafs when the team won its first Stanley Cup in 1931–32?

6) After losing the first three games of the 1942 Stanley Cup finals to Detroit, Leafs coach Hap Day decided to bench two of his best regulars, who were not producing in that series. The move paid off: the Leafs came back to win the Stanley Cup by taking the next four games. Who were the two players that were benched?

7) Prior to developing the Maple Leafs organization, Conn Smythe managed another NHL team. After one year of solid recruiting, Smythe was fired. He came home to Toronto, where he began the Maple Leafs dynasty. What team let Smythe go?

8) In the mid-1940s a line was put together that became known as "The Second Kid Line." What three players made up this trio?

9) In the mid-1940s, the Leafs assembled a line that became known as the "Flying Forts" because all three players came from the town of Fort William, Ontario. Who were the three players?

The members of the Maple Leafs' famous "Kid Line" (see question 3).

Goaltender Walter "Turk" Broda makes a save.

10) From 1947 to 1949, the Maple Leafs won three consecutive Stanley Cups. Three players scored the Stanley Cup–winning goals. Can you name them?

11) Prior to the building of Maple Leaf Gardens in 1931, where did the Leafs play their home games?

12) True or false? The Maple Leafs are the only team to have finished fourth in the final standings in the six-team league and yet to have won the Stanley Cup.

13) How many times have the Maple Leafs had the best overall regular-season record in the NHL since 1927?

Leafs centre Ted Kennedy is on the edge of the crease in front of Boston goalie Jim Henry. The other Leaf is Sid Smith.

14) On October 16, 1946, Gordie Howe scored his first NHL goal in his first game. The opposition that night was the Toronto Maple Leafs. Who was the Leafs goalie that allowed Howe's first goal?

15) Who was the first coach of the Toronto Maple Leafs in 1926–27?

16) Who was the first Leafs goalie to receive a penalty, and what was unusual about it?

17) Against what team did the Maple Leafs earn their first home ice win at Maple Leaf Gardens?

18) The 48th Highlanders have been a tradition on opening night at Maple Leaf Gardens, and now at the Air Canada Centre since the 1931–32 season. The marching band was there the night the Gardens opened, November 12, 1931. What song did they play that night?

19) A phrase uttered by Conn Smythe became as famous as he was. In fact, this saying became the rallying cry of the Leafs. What was that saying?

20) On opening night for the 1951–52 season, the Leafs met the Chicago Blackhawks at the Gardens on October 13, 1951. Conn Smythe had two royal guests watching the game with him. Who were they?

21) Which Leafs goalie allowed three consecutive Stanley Cup–winning goals in 1938, 1939 and 1940?

22) Foster Hewitt was largely responsible for bringing Maple Leafs hockey to fans across Canada via his radio broadcasts. It is said that Hewitt made the Maple Leafs a national institution. What was the introduction Foster Hewitt originally used to start his broadcast?

23) Bill Hewitt followed in his father's footsteps when he started on the television broadcasts of Maple Leafs games. When did Bill Hewitt first start his broadcasting career?

24) John Arnott was a great Leafs fan who was well known at Maple Leaf Gardens for leading a cheer. This cheer was used in trying to encourage a particular Leafs player. What was the cheer and who was the player?

25) Leafs general manager Conn Smythe had a long-running feud with the general manager of the Boston Bruins of the same era. Each would do whatever possible to get the upper hand and infuriate the other manager. One time, while in Beantown in the 1930s, Smythe took out an ad in a Boston newspaper proclaiming, "Attention Hockey Fans! If you're tired of seeing the kind of hockey the Boston Bruins are playing, come to the

Toronto forward Harry Watson attacks the New York net blocked by goalie Gump Worsley.

Garden[s] tonight and see a real hockey club, the Toronto Maple Leafs!" Needless to say, the Boston general manager was furious. Who was he?

26) In the 1951 playoffs, the Leafs met the Boston Bruins in the semi-finals. On Saturday, March 31, 1951, the Leafs and Bruins battled to a 1–1 tie in regulation time. After 20 minutes of overtime the game was stopped and there was no winner declared. Can you explain why?

27) In the 1947 Stanley Cup finals, Toronto defeated Montreal 4 games to 2. The Leafs clinched the series on home ice, but the Stanley Cup was not presented in front of the Maple Leaf Gardens crowd. The Cup had been left back in Montreal. Who had ordered this and why?

Max Bentley, Fern Flaman and Foster Hewitt

Bill and Foster Hewitt

28) The Maple Leafs did not play in the Stanley Cup finals in 1950. However, because one of the teams involved in the series could not use its home rink, two games were played at Maple Leaf Gardens. Who were the teams and which rink was unavailable?

29) Why did Conn Smythe select the nickname "Maple Leafs"?

30) The career of one of the Maple Leafs' first great players ended suddenly in Boston on December 12, 1933. Irwin "Ace" Bailey was hit so viciously from behind by a Bruin that

he was knocked unconscious and nearly died. Although he recovered, Bailey never played again. To honor Bailey, the Leafs retired his sweater, number 6, and played a benefit game for him and his family on February 12, 1934: the Leafs played against a group of NHL All-Star players at Maple Leaf Gardens. Who was the Bruin player that checked Bailey and what was the result of this unofficial All-Star Game?

31) When Punch Imlach first took on the job of coaching the Maple Leafs, whom did he replace?
Hint: This man went on to coach the Chicago Blackhawks and took that team to the Stanley Cup finals on three occasions, only to lose each time to the Montreal Canadiens.

32) During the 1959–60 season, the Leafs had a line known as "The Rocks." It was a fourth line whose main task was to rattle the opposition. Can you name the three rambunctious individuals who made up this line?

Red Kelly (#4) and goalie Bruce Gamble (#1) defend against Montreal's Dick Duff.

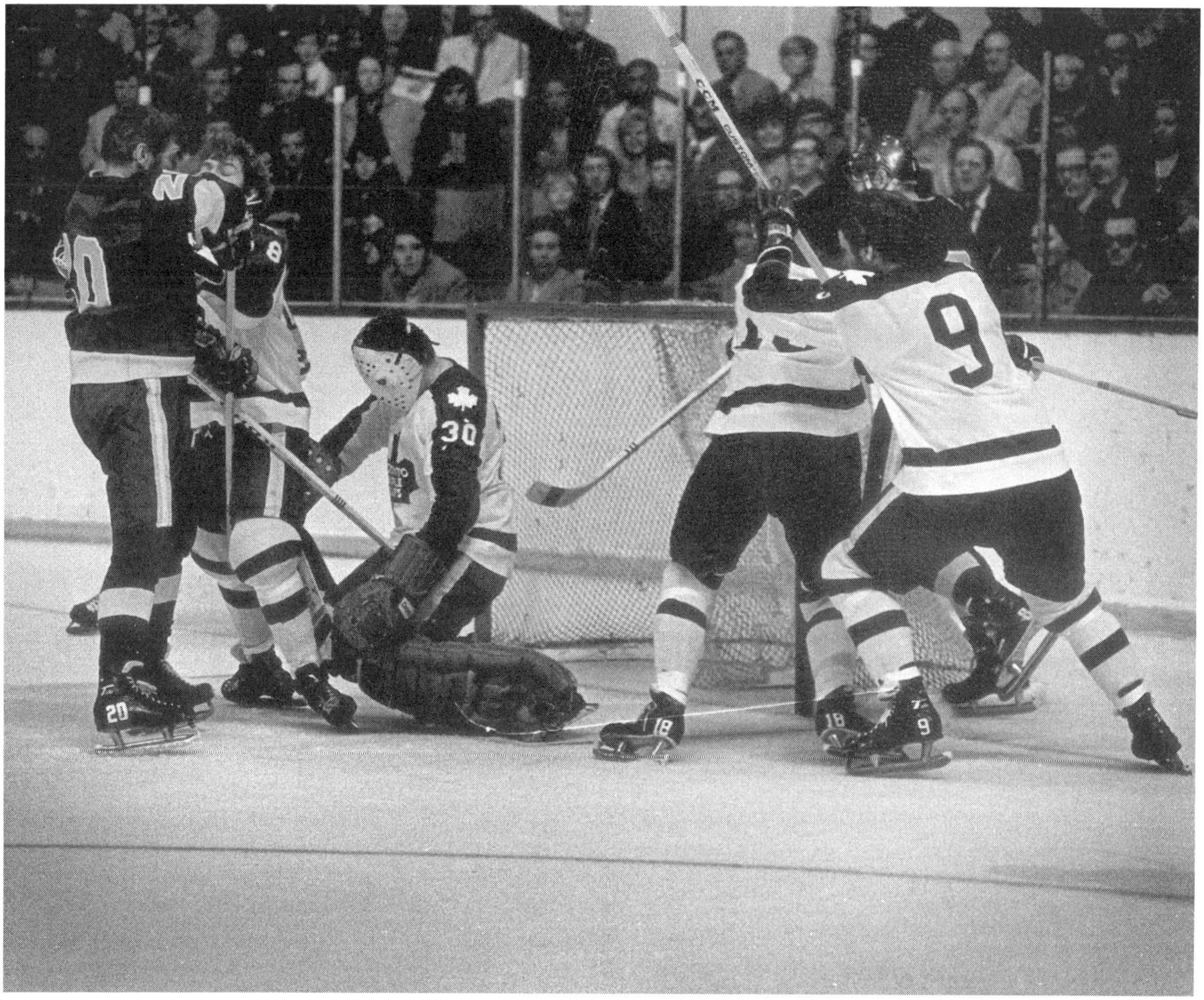

Goaltender Bernie Parent (#30) makes a save against the Los Angeles Kings.

33) In October 1962, Jim Norris, then president of the Chicago Blackhawks, offered the Maple Leafs a million dollars for one hockey player. The Leafs, represented by Harold Ballard, accepted at first, but later backed out of the deal and returned the cheque to a disgusted Norris. Can you name the player involved in this "transaction"?

34) During the 1960s, Punch Imlach built a very good farm system that provided a steady source of players to Toronto. However, by 1968, the board of directors of Maple Leaf Gardens decided to sell two vital teams in the Leafs farm system, which precipitated a decline in the team's fortunes in the late 1960s and on into the 1970s. Can you name the two minor-league teams that were sold?

Ron Ellis (#8) scores on Montreal's Gump Worsley.

35) From 1962 to 1965, one Leaf served as a member of the federal Parliament in Ottawa. Along with his playing duties, he represented the riding of York West for two terms as a member of the Liberals. He became known as the "Member for Centre Ice." Can you name him?
Hint: He went on to coach three NHL teams, including the Leafs.

36) When the Leafs acquired Bernie Parent, their goaltending problems appeared to be solved. However, when the WHA was formed, Parent decided to leave Toronto and join the new league. Parent played for the Philadelphia Blazers during his short WHA career. However, the Blazers were not the team that Parent originally signed with in the WHA. Can you name the team that Parent signed with but never played for?
Hint: This team never did play in the WHA because the franchise never got off the ground.

37) Three Leafs (1972–73 team) were selected for the 1972 Team Canada that defeated the Russians on Paul Henderson's dramatic goal. Paul Henderson is of course the most well known, but can you name the other two Leafs chosen? *Hint: One played on Henderson's line and had the job of checking Valeri Kharlamov. The other, a defenceman, never did see any action against the Russians.*

38) Four other members of the 1972 edition of Team Canada at one time or another wore a Leafs uniform during their NHL careers. Two were forwards, one was a goalie and the fourth was a defenceman. Can you name them?

39) Before losing to the New York Islanders in 1981, the Leafs had won five consecutive preliminary round playoff series. Can you name all the teams the Leafs beat in the elimination round? *Hint: There are only three teams to be named.*

Paul Henderson (#19) had 38 goals for the Leafs in 1971–72.

40) The Philadelphia Flyers were well known for playing Kate Smith's "God Bless America" before home games as a good luck charm. To counteract this during the 1975–76 quarter-finals against Philadelphia, Leafs coach Red Kelly decided to use a gimmick of his own to stifle old Kate. Can you remember what it was?
Hint: The real things are found in the Egyptian desert!

Lanny McDonald

41) During the 1970s, the Toronto Marlboros junior team won the Memorial Cup twice—in 1972–73 and 1974–75. Despite the fact that the Leafs did not sponsor the Marlies as they once had, a total of five players from those championship teams went on to play in the NHL for Toronto. Can you name the five players?
Hint: Two were centres, one was a defenceman, one a left winger, and one a goalie. Four were draft choices, while the other was acquired through a trade.

42) During the All-Star break of February 1979, the NHL All-Stars played the Soviet Union in the Challenge Cup. The Russians trounced the NHL team in the third and final game 6–0 to take the series 2 games to 1. Three members of the 1978–79 Maple Leafs were selected for the NHL team. All three played in every game. Can you name the Leafs players chosen?

43) In November 1961, Conn Smythe finally agreed to sell the Maple Leafs and Maple Leaf Gardens—the team and rink he had built

Harold Ballard (left) rides in a car with captain George Armstrong (middle), fellow owner Stafford Smythe and the 1967 Stanley Cup.

himself. The purchase was made by a group of three men who took charge of all Leafs operations. Can you name them?

44) Before the 1972–73 season began, the Leafs roster was decimated by the rival WHA, who signed away disgruntled players, leaving many big gaps on the team that could not be filled. A total of five players who were with Toronto in 1971–72 jumped to the new league when Harold Ballard refused to get involved in a bidding war. Can you name the five players?

45) The Leafs have not had very many American-born players play for them until recent years. Between 1970 and 1979, for example, only four U.S.-born players put on Leafs colours. Can you name them?
Hint: Three were forwards and one was a defenceman. Some of these names are very obscure, so if you name all these players you are a true Leafs fan!

46) King Clancy was coach of the Maple Leafs back in the mid-1950s. However, he also did some coaching during the '60s and '70s when the team's regular coaches were ailing. Can you name the years in which Clancy filled in and who he was temporarily replacing?

King Clancy

47) In 1976, the Canada Cup tournament saw one of the greatest gatherings of hockey talent. Four members of the 1976–77 Toronto Maple Leafs played in that tournament. Can you name them?
Hint: They were not all on Team Canada.

48) Two of the Maple Leafs chosen to play in the 1976 Canada Cup were named to the tournament's All-Star Team. Name both players.

49) Four players named to the original lineup of Team Canada for the 1976 Canada Cup played for the Leafs at one time during their NHL careers but were not with Toronto in 1976. None of the four played in any games for Canada. Can you name them?

50) Of the six men who coached the Leafs in the years 1970 to 1981, three played for Toronto during the 1960s. Can you name them?

51) Only one Leafs coach has ever had his own son play for the team while he was behind the bench. Can you name the player and coach?

52) In 1974, a team comprising WHA players met the Soviet Union in an eight-game series. Although this team put up a valiant effort, the Russians had enough power to subdue the WHA team. Seven members of this Team Canada were former Maple Leafs. Can you name them?
Hint: One was a goaltender, two were defencemen and four were forwards. Two of the forwards were also members of the 1972 Team Canada.

53) No NHL All-Star Team has been made up of members from only one team. The Chicago Blackhawks almost did it in the 1963–64

George "Punch" Imlach ran the Maple Leafs from 1958 to 1969 and won four Stanley Cups during that time.

Tim Horton (#7) watches Jean Ratelle of the New York Rangers.

season, when they held five of the six positions on the first All-Star Team. The only player to break the Chicago sweep was a Leaf. Can you name him?

54) The Kansas City Scouts (who later became the Colorado Rockies) first started their hockey operations for the 1974–75 season. The first amateur draft choice they ever made (second overall in the 1974 draft behind their expansion cousins, the Washington Capitals) later went on to play for the Maple Leafs. Can you name him?

55) When Punch Imlach returned to the Leafs in the 1979–80 season, it was a year filled with controversy. The controversy started even before the playing season began, as Imlach was determined to keep two players from performing in *Showdown*, a skills competition television series. He went so far as to take the matter to court in order to get an injunction against the two. The players won the case, but a deep rift between Imlach and the two Maple Leafs stars developed. Can you name the two players involved?

Doug Gilmour was great at setting up plays from anywhere on the ice.

56) The NHL All-Star Game has gone through many different formats. During the 1960s, the Stanley Cup champions would play a group of All-Stars chosen from the league's other teams. The Leafs faced an NHL All-Star Team four times between 1962 and 1968. What was the Leafs' won–lost record in those encounters?

57) True or false? During the Leafs' string of three consecutive Stanley Cup championships between 1962 and 1964, they did not have the leading playoff scorer in any of those years.

58) The last time a Toronto Maple Leaf won the Art Ross Trophy as the leading scorer during the regular season was in 1938. The closest the Leafs have come to this award since 1960 is two third-place finishes by two players. Who are the two players and in what seasons did they obtain their third-place standing? *Hint: Both players wore the same sweater number.*

59) True or false? After the Leafs won the Stanley Cup in 1967, they missed the playoffs in 1967–68 despite the fact that they had a *better* record than in the year they won the championship—more points, more goals for and fewer goals against.

60) The last time the Leafs won the Stanley Cup, in 1967, they used five different goaltenders during the season. Johnny Bower and Terry Sawchuk are probably the first to come to mind, but can you name the other three?

61) The Ontario attorney general became involved in hockey violence after an incident at Maple Leaf Gardens in November 1975. One player who was then with the Detroit Red Wings was charged and later tried for his assault on a Leafs player during an NHL game in Toronto. He was subsequently cleared of all charges and the Leafs later acquired him in a very controversial trade with the Red Wings. Can you name him, the player he assaulted and the player the Leafs gave up to Detroit to get him?

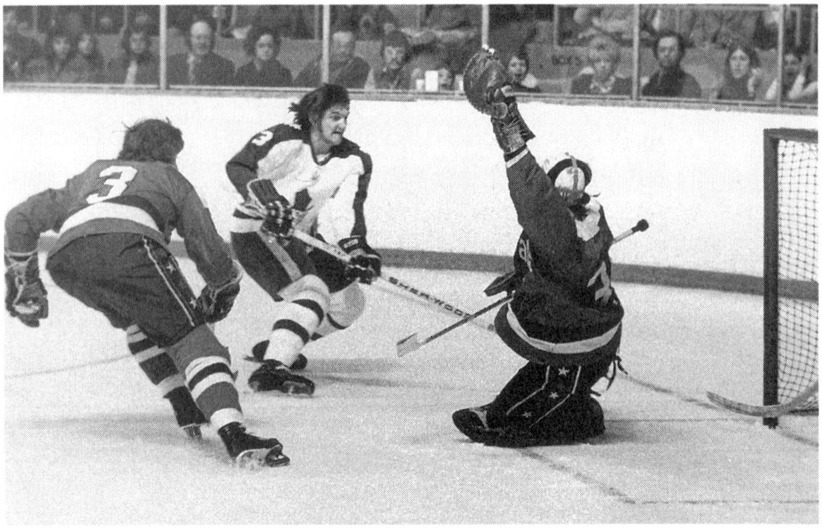

Bob Neely tries to score on the Washington Capitals.

62) One Leafs forward was charged in court by the Ontario attorney general after his stick cut Pittsburgh's Dennis Owchar in the head, requiring 25 stitches, in a 1977 game in Toronto. However, the Leafs player was cleared of all charges. Can you name the Leaf involved?

Johnny Bower stops Paul Henderson of Detroit.

63) Can you name the goaltending victims of the winning goals the Leafs scored on the nights they won the Stanley Cup in 1962, 1963, 1964 and 1967?

Al Iafrate was a first-round draft choice by the Leafs.

Dave Williams once held the team record for most career penalty minutes.

John Anderson (#10) scores against the New York Rangers.

64) Many teams made a big mistake by passing on the opportunity to draft Bobby Clarke in 1969. The Philadelphia Flyers picked Clarke with their second choice (17th overall) in the 1969 draft. The Leafs, like several other teams, did not take Clarke in the first round although the opportunity existed, because they had the ninth choice overall. Can you name the player Toronto picked as its first choice in the 1969 amateur draft?
Hint: He has never played a game for the Leafs or in the NHL.

65) A former first-round draft choice of Vancouver, this winger once scored 40 goals in one season (1978–79) for the Canucks. He played one season for the Leafs (1980–81) and scored 10 goals in 21 games for the club. Can you name him?
Hint: He played in Chicago between his stays in Vancouver and Toronto.

66) The New York Islanders used their first draft selection of 1977 to take Mike Bossy from the Laval Nationals. Bossy was the 15th player chosen overall, meaning many teams passed on the 50-goal sniper. The Leafs had the 11th and 12th picks in the 1977 draft, but they did not select Bossy. Can you name the two players the Leafs did draft?

Howie Meeker behind the bench

Bob Pulford (#20) battles Bill Gadsby of Detroit.

67) The Maple Leafs are not the only team to have problems with their first-round draft choices. The Atlanta Flames (who have since moved to Calgary) are a good example. In both 1975 and 1976, the Flames had the eighth pick overall and chose a defenceman in each case. Both these players would be elsewhere by 1980 and they would both play for Toronto. Can you name them?

68) Right winger Ron Ellis wore sweater number 6 (which had been retired) for most of his career with the Leafs; he was given the number by its previous wearer, Ace Bailey. Ellis wore two other sweater numbers in his career as a Leaf. What were the other two numbers?

Bob Baun (#21) keeps a close eye on John Ferguson of the Canadiens.

69) Harold Ballard was never an owner to hide his feelings. In 1974–75, he was very outspoken when the team was not playing up to expectations. According to Ballard, who "could go into the corner with six eggs in his pocket and not break one of them"?

70) Which Leafs coach was supposedly "fired" on a Thursday night (after a 2–1 loss to Montreal) only to be "re-hired" on the Saturday of the same week, making a dramatic entrance into Maple Leaf Gardens just before the start of a game against the Philadelphia Flyers? (The Leafs defeated Philadelphia in that game 4–3.)
Hint: The Toronto players had requested that Ballard "reconsider" his decision to fire the coach in question.

71) One of the few Leafs players to wear sweater number 27, this one-time Leafs coach also had a brother who was an outstanding lineman for the Toronto Argonauts of the Canadian Football League. Can you name him?

The Maple Leafs' 1967 Stanley Cup team

72) The Leafs teams of the 1960s were known as "clutch and grab" artists. However, one Leafs defenceman gave the term new meaning when he wore palmless gloves. This enabled him to put his fingers through the holes and grab opponents' sweaters—a big advantage when he was trying to control the opposition in front of the net. When a referee discovered his innovation, a league rule was passed banning palmless gloves. Can you name this inventive Toronto defenceman?

73) The only two sweater numbers the Leafs have ever retired are those of Bill Barilko, who wore number 5 (he died in a plane crash in the summer of 1951), and Ace Bailey, who wore number 6 (his career ended in 1933, during a game). Eight former Leafs have had their sweater numbers retired by another team. Who are the players, what are the retired numbers and by which teams were they retired?

Johnny Bower (#1) stops the Detroit Red Wings in the 1964 Stanley Cup finals.

74) Who holds the Leafs record for most points in a season by a rookie?

75) Despite success with Team Canada in 1972, Paul Henderson and the Leafs parted company in 1974. Henderson made the jump to the rival WHA, but would return to the NHL as a member of the Atlanta Flames. Which WHA team did Henderson sign with when he decided to leave the Leafs?
Hint: The team Henderson signed with would move to a new location in 1976.

76) The following were nicknames of former Leafs players:
a) "Shaky"
b) "Howie"
c) "Boomer"
d) "Waldo"
e) "Spinner"
Can you identify each player?

77) One of the very few goaltenders to win the Hart Trophy as the NHL's most valuable player, this goalie won the award in 1962 and later played for the Leafs. Can you name him?

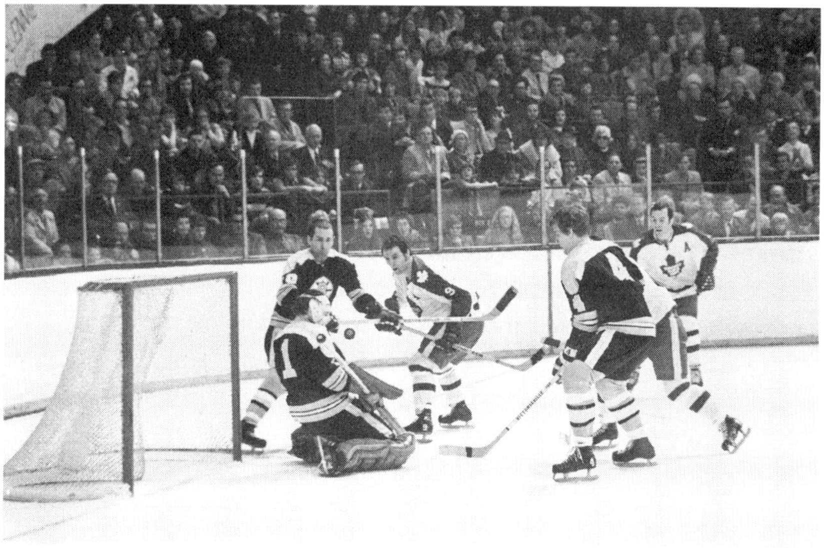

Norm Ullman (#9) looks for a rebound against the Bruins.

Mike Walton (#16) made a strong contribution to the Leafs during the 1967 playoffs.

78) The first-ever NHL goal to be scored on a penalty shot in the Stanley Cup playoffs was allowed by a one-time Leafs goaltender. Can you name the goaltender and the team he was with at the time?

79) Many well-known entertainers have become hockey fans, especially since Los Angeles received an NHL franchise. One well-known celebrity, famous for his "Tiptoe Through the Tulips" and for getting married on Johnny Carson's *Tonight Show,* was a long-time Leafs fan and supporter. Can you name him?

80) Which Leafs player once had a song written about him that made the top of the local record charts?

81) One Leaf tried his hand at singing. In fact, he once put out a Christmas song entitled "Honky the Christmas Goose." Can you name this singing Leafs player?

82) Maple Leaf Gardens was home to the Leafs from 1931 to 1999. However, on March 7, 1968, it became "home" for another NHL team because that team's arena roof had fallen in. The game was marred by an ugly incident

Tim Horton (#7), Frank Mahovlich and Dave Keon attack the Canadiens net.

Eddie Shack returned to the Leafs for the 1973–74 season.

involving a former Leaf. Who was the "home" team and who were the players involved in the vicious stick-swinging incident?

83) Dave Hodge was an outstanding host for Leafs television broadcasts beginning in the 1971–72 season, when he took over from a long-time host who had departed for England to take a government position. Can you name the man Dave Hodge replaced on *Hockey Night in Canada*?

Nik Antropov

84) A former Calder Trophy winner who once coached the Leafs also became a member of Parliament in Ottawa. He was well known across Canada in the 1970s for his energetic analysis of hockey games on *Hockey Night in Canada*. Can you name him?
Hint: He scored five goals in one game as a rookie on January 8, 1947, during a 10–4 win by the Leafs over Chicago.

85) This Leafs defenceman played with Toronto during the 1940s, when he shared in two Stanley Cup victories. The Leafs sent him on to Chicago in a trade and the Blackhawks dealt him to Detroit where he was a part of three more championships with the Red Wings. During the 1960s and 1970s he served as a colour commentator and analyst for Maple Leafs television broadcasts on *Hockey Night in Canada*. Who was he?

86) After a great junior career with the Toronto Marlboros, this former NHL defenceman was the number-one draft selection of the Vancouver Canucks in 1970—the year they started their franchise. However, after only three seasons he was dealt away. He was traded again before his career ended. The other two teams he played for were the Chicago Blackhawks and the Pittsburgh Penguins. After his playing days were over he turned to broadcasting, and became the colour man on Maple Leafs radio broadcasts midway through the 1980–81 season. Can you name him?

87) During his playing career with the Maple Leafs, defenceman Carl Brewer wore three sweater numbers. What were they?

Tomas Kaberle

88) Since 1969, four first-overall entry draft selections went on to play for the Leafs, although none of them was originally drafted by Toronto. Can you name them all?
Hint: One was a centre taken by Detroit, another was a winger drafted by the New York Islanders and two were selected by Quebec.

89) Few players have worn sweater number 27 for the Leafs. Can you name the last five players to do so?

90) From 1981 to 1983 the junior Western Hockey League's award for top defenceman went to a player chosen by the Maple Leafs in the entry draft. Can you name the three award recipients?

91) The 1967 Maple Leafs Stanley Cup–winning team featured many players who were in the twilight of their careers. In fact, many of them retired shortly thereafter. However, one player on that team continued playing until 1982, making him the last player from the 1967 Cup team to retire. Who was he?
Hint: He finished his NHL career with the Hartford Whalers.

92) Before the start of the 1976–77 season, the Kansas City Scouts moved to Denver, Colorado, and became known as the Colorado Rockies. Their first home game was played at the McNichols Sports Arena in Denver against the Toronto Maple Leafs. What was the outcome?

93) Between 1979 and 1983, the Maple Leafs lost 12 consecutive playoff games before finally winning a post-season game on April 9, 1983. The Leafs lost those 12 consecutive games to three different teams. Can you name the three teams and the team the Leafs beat to end the streak?

94) In the 1984 entry draft the Leafs had the fourth choice overall. The player chosen was born in the United States, making him the first American-born player to be chosen by the Leafs with their first selection. Can you name him?

95) Darryl Sittler was chosen by the Leafs in the first round of the 1970 amateur draft. He was taken eighth overall. A teammate of Sittler's with the London Knights was also chosen in the first round by Chicago, but eventually played with the Leafs some years later. Who was he?

96) World Hockey Association owner Johnny Bassett brought hockey to the southern United States with his team the Birmingham Bulls. Prior to the 1979–80 season, Bassett signed junior players who were still eligible to play in junior but not yet old enough to be drafted by the NHL as the rules stood then. These players became known as the "Baby Bulls." Three of these players went on to play for the Maple Leafs. Can you name them?
Hint: Two were defencemen and the third was a right winger. All were acquired in trades.

97) What was the highest number ever worn by a Leaf and which player wore it?

98) In June 1985, the Maple Leafs had the number-one choice overall in the entry draft for the first time since the universal draft started. What player did the Leafs select and what was his junior team?

Leafs captain Mats Sundin was named an NHL second team All-Star for his performance in the 2001–02 season.

99) After an excellent season with the Victoria Cougars of the WHL (Western Hockey League), this centre was the Leafs' first draft choice (seventh overall) in the 1983 draft. Before he played for Toronto he was a member of the 1984 Canadian Olympic hockey team. Can you name him?

100) A former Atlanta Flames 1978 second-round draft choice ended up providing the Maple Leafs with solid goaltending in the last half of the 1984–85 season. Up to that point, his previous NHL experience had been six games with the Calgary Flames. Who was he?

Tom Fitzgerald

101) During the 1979–80 season the Leafs had three men coach the team behind the bench during games. The general manager named himself coach midway through the season but never went behind the bench for any games. Can you name the four people involved in this unusual situation?

102) In May 1957 a hockey committee was established to run the Maple Leafs and the Gardens. This group was to be a policy-developing committee designed to take many of the administrative duties away from Conn Smythe. The group was essentially made up of sports-minded businessmen and included Harold Ballard. By what name was this group known?

103) A one-time Leafs goaltender was named rookie of the year in three professional hockey leagues. The goalie was rookie of the year in Omaha in the United States Hockey League (1948), in Indianapolis in the American Hockey League (1949) and in the NHL (1951). Can you name him?

104) For the 1967–68 season the NHL expanded to 12 teams from 6. Two six-team divisions were created: the Eastern Division for the old established clubs and the Western Division for the six new entries. The Western Division's leading scorer for the year was a former Maple Leaf. Who was he and what team did he play for?

105) Bobby Orr was the NHL rookie of the year for 1967. A Leafs player finished third behind Orr and Ed Van Impe in the voting for the Calder Trophy. Who was he?

106) During the years that Punch Imlach coached the Leafs, how many times did the team win a seventh game to capture a playoff series? What was the overall record in the seventh-game showdowns during the Imlach era?

107) In the 1967–68 season, what team became the first expansion team to play in Maple Leaf Gardens (on October 25, 1967)?

108) Alan Eagleson was instrumental in establishing the NHL Players Association (NHLPA). He was the NHLPA's first executive director. A Leafs player was named as the first president of the NHLPA. Who was he?

109) After the 1974–75 season, Dave Keon left the Leafs for the World Hockey Association. Which WHA team did Keon play for in 1975–76?

110) Bobby Orr played in his first All-Star Game against the Maple Leafs in 1968, earning one assist. What uniform number did he wear in that game?

111) Bobby Hull, Al Secord and Jeremy Roenick are the only Chicago Blackhawks to have scored 50 goals in one season. Hull scored 50 goals five times, Secord did it once and Roenick hit the magic number twice. Leafs goaltenders have been the victim for all three of these players on at least one occasion when they scored their 50th. Can you name the goalies?

Goaltender Trevor Kidd

112) In 1978, Leafs owner Harold Ballard feuded with NHL president John Ziegler about the rule requiring player names to be put on the back of the sweaters. Ballard said this would hurt program sales. Eventually Ballard agreed to abide by the rules. He placed the names on the Leafs sweaters for a game in Chicago, but what Ballard did was not exactly what Ziegler had in mind. What had Ballard done?

113) Which former Leafs defenceman coached the Toronto Toros of the WHA in 1975–76?

114) One-time Leafs goalie Jacques Plante was the first goalie to use a face mask on a regular basis in the modern era. While with Montreal he used it in practice and finally wore it in a game against the New York Rangers on November 1, 1959, when he stopped a shot in the face and was cut. Plante agreed to return to the net only after coach Toe Blake gave him permission to use a mask. The player who took the shot was a future Leaf. Who was he?

115) The year 1967 marked Canada's 100th birthday and the country celebrated Centennial Year with many events and festivities. In keeping with the spirit of that year, the Leafs changed their playoff uniforms. The change

proved to be lucky: the Leafs won the Cup. What was the change?

116) What was the slogan in the Leafs dressing room during the glory years of the 1960s?

117) On April 3, 1966, in a game against the Red Wings in Detroit, the Leafs used three goalies—one of the few times this has happened in the NHL. Who were the goalies?

118) A goaltender who shared the Vezina Trophy in 1980, and who made the NHL second All-Star Team in 1978 and 1980, was acquired by the Maple Leafs during the summer of 1985 from the Calgary Flames. Can you name him?

119) Who won the World Hockey Association coach of the year honours in 1978–79 while coaching the Birmingham Bulls?

120) Which former Maple Leafs player was awarded the Bill Masterton Trophy in 1983? *Hint: He holds the Calgary Flames record for most goals in one season—66.*

121) What was goaltender Johnny Bower the first to accomplish on March 26, 1963, in a semi-final playoff game against Montreal?

122) During the 1970s it was a popular trend for goalies to paint their masks. One of the first Leafs goalies to paint his mask was Doug Favell. What did Favell paint on his mask?

123) What junior team did Tim Horton, Frank Mahovlich, Dick Duff and Dave Keon all graduate to the Leafs from?

124) On November 1, 1952, a Maple Leafs game was televised (on the CBC) for the first time. Who did the Leafs play that night and what was the result?

125) Which Montreal Canadiens superstar was the first to shatter the Herculite glass in Maple Leaf Gardens after being checked?

126) What controversial event concerning the expansion of seating in Maple Leaf Gardens was Harold Ballard referring to when he said, "she doesn't pay me anything . . . besides, what position can she play?"

127) The Maple Leafs were awarded the O'Brien Trophy for the 1932–33 season. What was the O'Brien Trophy awarded for?

128) On February 17, 1927, Toronto's NHL hockey team skated out for the first time as the "Maple Leafs." Who did they play and what was the final score?

129) Prior to the start of the 1967 Stanley Cup finals, Punch Imlach declared that the Montreal Canadiens would never beat his Leafs "with a junior B goaltender." Who was the goaltender Imlach ridiculed?

130) The 1950–51 season marked the first time that the Leafs had two players who scored 30 goals or more in the same season. Who were the two players?

131) Who was the first Leaf to score
a) 100 career goals?
b) 200 career goals?
c) 300 career goals?

132) The last time a Detroit Red Wing led the NHL in goals scored was in 1964–65, when a centreman scored 42 times. He was acquired by the Leafs four years later in a trade. Who is he?

133) In the expansion draft of 1967, the Los Angeles Kings had the first selection among goaltenders. They took the Leafs netminder, who had sealed Toronto's 1967 Stanley Cup win with two victories over the Montreal Canadiens. Who was he and which players did coach Punch Imlach send out to protect him and a 2–1 lead on May 2, 1967, the night the Leafs won the Cup?

134) In 1986–87 the Leafs had their first black player. Aside from seven games played in the NHL with Buffalo, he had been a career minor leaguer. He played in only four games with Toronto. Can you name him?

135) True or false?
The Leafs were the first team in NHL history to win the Stanley Cup in three consecutive years.

136) What team have the Maple Leafs defeated most often in the Stanley Cup finals?

137) During the 1986–87 season the Leafs wore a patch on their uniforms to honor one of the great all-time Leafs. This former player also coached the team and was a long-time vice-president for the club. The patch featured a shamrock with a king's crown on top. Who was the honored person?

138) In 1985–86, a then record four American-born players were members of the same Leafs team. Can you name the players and the states in which they were born?

139) The 1984–85 American Hockey League rookie of the year played on the Leafs' farm club, the St. Catharines Saints. In 1985–86 he finally stuck with the Leafs and turned in a fine rookie year. In fact, he led the team in playoff scoring with 14 points. Who is he?

140) In the 1986 playoffs, the Leafs played surprisingly well, upsetting Chicago and nearly defeating St. Louis. A key ingredient in their success was "The Hound Line." Which three players made up this exciting trio?

141) The 1987 Canada Cup tournament was one of the most exciting international competitions ever staged. The Canadian team edged the Soviets two games to one in the finals with a goal late in the third game by Mario Lemieux. One Leafs player was asked to try out for Team Canada, although he did not make the final roster. Who is he?

142) Prior to a game with the St. Louis Blues on February 27, 1988, at Maple Leaf Gardens, the Leafs honored one of their all-time great players with a ceremony and gifts. It was the first time since 1977 the Leafs had paid formal tribute to a player. Who is the player the Leafs honored?

143) In order to help the Canadian Olympic hockey team in the 1988 Winter Olympics in Calgary, a few Canadian-based NHL teams offered players from their rosters to the squad. The Leafs sent one player to the Olympic Games. Who is he?

144) During their 1988 playoff series against Detroit, the Leafs faced their first penalty shot during the post-season. The shot was awarded during the fourth game of the series at Maple Leaf Gardens. Who were the shooter and goaltender involved, and what was the result?

145) In 1987–88 the Leafs endured one of their worst seasons ever, which led to the much-needed firing of general manager Gerry McNamara on February 7, 1988. To finish the season Harold Ballard appointed a three-man committee to look after the entire operation of the hockey team. Who were the three men selected?

146) A one-time captain of the Toronto Marlboros who went on to play for the New York Rangers and the Los Angeles Kings (scoring one overtime-winning goal against Toronto in the 1975 playoffs) was named coach of the Maple Leafs in 1996. Can you name him?

147) A former mentor of the University of Toronto hockey teams, this coach was with the Calgary Flames when they won the Stanley Cup in 1989. He came to the Leafs as an assistant to Doug Carpenter for the 1990–91 season and was named head coach after just 11 games. Can you name him?

148) Former Toronto first-round draft choices have led both the Maple Leafs and the Montreal Canadiens in scoring for one season. Can you name these two players?

149) This smallish winger played an effective role for the Leafs during the 1991–92 season after he was picked up in a minor-league deal. His father once played in the NHL with Montreal, and he wore sweater number 11 for the Leafs, just like his dad had for the Habs. He became a crowd favourite, prompting fans to adopt the chant "Guy, Guy." Who was this much-travelled player?

150) February 25, 1993, was a big night for Leafs rookie goalie Felix Potvin, when he faced the Montreal Canadiens on home ice for the first time. At the opposite end of the ice was his childhood hero Patrick Roy. What was the result of the game?

151) Acquired in a deal with Hartford in 1992 for a second-round draft choice, this centre played for the Leafs just like his father Barry did in the 1950s. Can you name him?

152) Which two Maple Leafs goaltending legends have had their sweater number 1 raised to the rafters as "honored" players?

153) Signed as a free agent in 1997, this native of Scarborough, Ontario, was trained at Bowling Green University and played over two seasons with the Leafs before he was dealt to the Tampa Bay Lightning for Darcy Tucker. Can you name him?

154) In Mike Smith's only draft as associate general manager with the Maple Leafs, a surprise selection was made with the 10th overall pick, when the team took a big player from Kazakhstan. This player would make the Leafs team in 1999–2000. Can you name him?

155) After 1,540 consecutive games, Toronto's distinctive public address announcer retired

Leafs coach Dick Irvin (left) and manager Conn Smythe pose for the camera.

prior to the start of the 1999–2000 season. Can you name him and his replacement?

156) Drafted 204th overall in 1996, this Leaf was the team's top-scoring defenceman in 1999–2000 with 40 points. Can you name him?

157) Only one player in NHL history has ever had two penalty shots in one Stanley Cup playoff year. It happened in 1999 to a Maple Leafs player. Can you name him and describe the results?

158) In 1995–96, Maple Leafs fans were asked to vote for an all-time Leafs team by position. Which players were chosen by the fans?

159) On July 4, 2000, the Maple Leafs announced the signing of two veteran players. Both said they had always wanted to play in Toronto and to put on Leafs sweaters. Name the players and the special sweater numbers they were given.

160) Signed as a free agent in 1996 by the Leafs, this large (6'4", 214 pounds) but soft right winger (he has scored 78 goals for the Leafs as of the end of the 2002–03 season) would have been dealt to another NHL team but for a mechanical malfunction. A fax machine jammed, a deadline was missed and the deal was nixed. Name the Leafs player, the team that was set to acquire him and the junior player Toronto was going to get in the trade.

161) On March 2, 2002, the Maple Leafs played their 75th anniversary game against the Buffalo Sabres at the Air Canada Centre (a 3–3 tie) and honored their top 25 players of all time. What else did the Maple Leafs do to celebrate the occasion? *Hint: It has to do with the team uniform.*

162) Drafted in 1990 (11th overall) by the Calgary Flames, who chose him ahead of such goalies as Felix Potvin and Martin Brodeur, this goaltender bounced around the

Goaltender Bernie Parent

Ron Ellis ("A" on sweater) scored 332 career goals as a Maple Leaf.

NHL (including stops in Carolina and Florida) before he signed on with the Leafs as a free agent in August of 2002. He posted a record of 6–10–2 in 19 appearances during the 2002–03 season. Name him.

163) The first captain of the Nashville Predators joined the Maple Leafs prior to the start of the 2002–03 season. He has also played for the New York Islanders, the Florida Panthers and the Chicago Blackhawks. Can you name this Massachusetts native?

164) When the Maple Leafs honored Darryl Sittler by raising his sweater number, 27, to the rafters at the Air Canada Centre during the 2002–03 season, his banner featured a special addition to it. What was it and why is it there?

165) Which Leafs player recorded his 1,000th career point (the fifth player to reach the milestone in a Toronto uniform) on March 10, 2003, during a 3–2 win over the Edmonton Oilers?

166) Who are the only two players in Leafs history to wear a sweater number in the 80s?
Hint: Both players were on the Leafs team of 2002–03.

167) When Phil Housley joined the Maple Leafs late in the 2002–03 season, he decided to wear sweater number 96. He became the fifth player in team history to wear a number in the 90s. Name the other four.

168) After a so-called exhaustive search for a new general manager in the summer of 2003, the Leafs finally settled on the son of a former well-known NHL enforcer as their man. Name him.
Hint: He was the Vice President and Director of Hockey Operations for the St. Louis Blues when the Leafs interviewed him for the position.

169) Just before the Maple Leafs opened training camp in September of 2003, they signed a veteran free agent centre who had been a Stanley Cup winner with New Jersey (2003), Dallas (1999) and Calgary (1989). Name him.

Inge Hammarstrom

Answers

1) The Toronto Arenas (who won the Stanley Cup in 1917–18) and the Toronto St. Pats (who won the Stanley Cup in 1921–22)
2) Hap Day was captain in 1932 and coached the team to Cup victories in 1942, 1945, 1947, 1948 and 1949.
3) Charlie Conacher, Joe Primeau and Harvey Jackson
4) The New York Rangers twice (1932–33 and 1939–40); the Montreal Maroons (1934–35); the Detroit Red Wings (1935–36); the Chicago Blackhawks (1937–38); the Boston Bruins (1938–39)
5) Conn Smythe was the general manager and Dick Irvin was the coach.
6) Gord Drillon and Bucko McDonald
7) The New York Rangers
8) Ted Kennedy, Howie Meeker and Vic Lynn
9) Gus Bodnar, Gaye Stewart and Bud Poile
10) 1947—Ted Kennedy; 1948—Harry Watson; 1949—Cal Gardner
11) Mutual Street Arena
12) True (1948–49)

Goalie Terry Sawchuk and teammates celebrate his 100th career shutout.

Carl Brewer

Brian Spencer (#15) tries to get away from Harry Howell of the Los Angeles Kings.

13) Four (1933–34; 1934–35; 1947–48; 1962–63)
14) Turk Broda
15) Alex Romeril
16) Lorne Chabot received the penalty and had to serve it himself in the penalty box! The Bruins scored three goals during the two minutes.
17) Toronto defeated the Boston Bruins 4–3 on November 28, 1931.
18) "Happy days are here again!"
19) "If you can't beat them in the alley, you can't beat them on the ice."
20) Princess Elizabeth (later to be Queen) and the Duke of Edinburgh (Prince Philip)
21) Turk Broda
22) "Hello Canada and hockey fans in the United States and Newfoundland."
23) As an eight-year-old, Bill Hewitt described part of a Leafs game on the radio on "Young Canada Night" in 1936.
24) The cheer was "Come on, Teeder" for Ted Kennedy.
25) Art Ross
26) Toronto city by-laws prohibited a sporting event from

Centre Russ Courtnall was a first-round draft choice of the Leafs.

continuing into the hours of Sunday morning. The Leafs won the series 4 games to 1 with one game tied.

27) Not wanting to be seen as overconfident and in fear of jinxing his team before the game, Leafs manager Conn Smythe had ordered that the Stanley Cup be left in Montreal.
28) The Detroit Red Wings and the New York Rangers. Madison Square Garden was unavailable.
29) He thought the maple leaf was a significant symbol across Canada, especially since the 1924 Canadian Olympic hockey team had worn maple leafs on their sweaters and because Smythe had worn maple leaf badges on his war uniform.
30) Eddie Shore hit Bailey. The Leafs won the game 7–3.
31) Billy Reay
32) Garry "Duke" Edmunston, Gerry James and Johnny Wilson
33) Frank Mahovlich
34) The Victoria Maple Leafs and the Rochester Americans
35) Red Kelly
36) Miami Screaming Eagles

Johnny Bower

Mats Sundin was named captain of the Leafs in 1996.

37) Ron Ellis and Brian Glennie
38) Frank Mahovlich, Jean-Paul Parise, Ed Johnston and Rod Seiling
39) The Los Angeles Kings (twice), the Pittsburgh Penguins (twice) and the Atlanta Flames
40) Kelly believed in "Pyramid Power." He ordered several pyramids to be installed under the Leafs bench and in the dressing room, then had the players sit, or put their sticks under them. Captain Darryl Sittler *did* score five goals in one playoff game after he put his sticks under a pyramid, but Kelly's scheme only lasted the 1976 playoff series against Philadelphia—which the Leafs lost.
41) From the 1972–73 team: Mike Palmateer. From the 1974–75 team: Bruce Boudreau, John Anderson, Trevor Johansen and Mike Kaszycki.
42) Lanny McDonald, Darryl Sittler and Borje Salming
43) Stafford Smythe, John Bassett and Harold Ballard
44) Bernie Parent, Ricky Ley, Brad Selwood, Jim Harrison and Guy Trottier
45) Gerry O'Flaherty, Dale Smedsmo, Tracy Pratt and Kurt Walker
46) In 1967 for Punch Imlach and in 1972 for John McClellan
47) Darryl Sittler and Lanny McDonald played for Canada, while Borje Salming and Inge Hammarstrom played for Sweden.
48) Darryl Sittler and Borje Salming
49) Gerry Cheevers, Dave Burrows, Dan Maloney and Rene Robert

Centre Nik Antropov changed sweater numbers near the end of the 2002–03 season.

50) Red Kelly, Floyd Smith and Joe Crozier (who played with the Leafs during 1959–60)
51) Brent Imlach, son of Punch Imlach, played for the Leafs during 1965–66 and 1966–67.
52) Gerry Cheevers, Rick Ley, Brad Selwood, Jim Harrison, Mike Walton, Frank Mahovlich and Paul Henderson
53) Tim Horton
54) Wilf Paiement
55) Darryl Sittler and Mike Palmateer
56) Toronto won two games, lost one and tied one.
Results:
1962—Toronto 4—All-Stars 1
1963—Toronto 3—All-Stars 3
1964—Toronto 2—All-Stars 3
1968—Toronto 4—All-Stars 3
57) True
58) Frank Mahovlich had 84 points during the 1960–61 season and Darryl Sittler had 117 points during the 1977–78 season, both good for third place in the Art Ross Trophy race in those years.
59) True

Alex Mogilny led the Leafs in points during the 2002–03 season.

60) Gary Smith (two games), Al Smith (one game) and Bruce Gamble (23 games)
61) Dan Maloney was the player charged for his attack on Leafs defenceman Brian Glennie. In March 1978, the Leafs gave up Errol Thompson and two draft choices to get Maloney.
62) Dave "Tiger" Williams
63) 1962—Chicago/Glenn Hall
1963—Detroit/Terry Sawchuk
1964—Detroit/Terry Sawchuk
1967—Montreal/Gump Worsley
64) Ernie Moser
65) Ron Sedlbauer
66) John Anderson and Trevor Johansen
67) Richard Mulhern and Dave Shand
68) Ellis wore numbers 8 and 11.
69) Inge Hammarstrom
70) Roger Neilson
71) Former Leafs coach Mike Nykoluk's brother Danny played for the Argos between 1957 and 1971.
72) Carl Brewer
73) Buffalo—number 2 for Tim Horton and number 14 for Rene Robert
Hartford—number 2 for Ricky Ley

Dave Keon was named one of the top 25 Maple Leafs of all time.

The other names on the Leafs' list of all time greatest players are: Syl Apps, George Armstrong, Max Bentley, Johnny Bower, Turk Broda, King Clancy, Charlie Conacher, Wendel Clark, Hap Day, Doug Gilmour, Tim Horton, Harvey Jackson, Red Kelly, Ted Kennedy, Frank Mahovlich, Lanny McDonald, Joe Primeau, Bob Pulford, Borje Salming, Allan Stanley, Darryl Sittler, Jim Thompson, Mats Sundin and Rick Vaive.

Philadelphia—number 1 for Bernie Parent
Calgary—number 9 for Lanny McDonald
Detroit—number 1 for Terry Sawchuk
Montreal—number 1 for Jacques Plante
Ottawa—number 8 for Frank Finnigan

74) Peter Ihnacak with 66 points in 1982–83
75) Paul Henderson signed with the Toronto Toros, who became the Birmingham Bulls.
76) a) Mike Walton
b) Jim McKenny
c) Bobby Baun
d) Bob Neely
e) Brian Spencer
77) Jacques Plante won the Hart Trophy in 1962 as a member of the Montreal Canadiens.
78) Terry Sawchuk, then with Los Angeles, allowed the goal scored by Wayne Connelly on April 9, 1968.
79) Tiny Tim
80) A song was written about Eddie Shack entitled "Clear the Track, Here Comes Shack."
81) Johnny Bower
82) The "home" team that night was the Philadelphia Flyers and the visitors were the Boston Bruins. The stick-swinging affair took place between Boston's Eddie Shack and Philadelphia's Larry Zeidel.
83) Ward Cornell
84) Howie Meeker
85) Bob Goldham
86) Dale Tallon
87) Carl Brewer wore numbers 18, 2 and 28.
88) Dale McCourt in 1977, Billy Harris in 1972 and Mats Sundin in 1989 and Owen Nolan in 1990.
89) Miroslav Ihnacak, Dave Semenko, John Kordic, Lucien DeBlois and Shayne Corson
90) Jim Benning, 1981; Gary Nylund, 1982; Gary Leeman, 1983
91) Dave Keon
92) Colorado Rockies 4, Maple Leafs 2
93) The Montreal Canadiens (1979, 4 games); the Minnesota North Stars (1980, 3 games); the New York Islanders (1981, 3 games) and Minnesota again (1983, 2 games) account for 12 straight playoff defeats. Toronto beat Minnesota 6–3 in the third game of the Norris Division semi-finals in 1983 to end the streak.
94) Al Iafrate
95) Dan Maloney was chosen 14th overall by Chicago in the first round of the 1970 draft.
96) Gaston Gingras, Rob Ramage and Rick Vaive
97) Wilf Paiement wore number 99.
98) Wendel Clark from the Saskatoon Blades
99) Russ Courtnall
100) Tim Bernhardt
101) Floyd Smith, Dick Duff and Joe Crozier all worked behind the bench. Punch Imlach was the coach who never worked behind the bench during a game.
102) "The Silver Seven"
103) Terry Sawchuk
104) Andy Bathgate of the Pittsburgh Penguins
105) Brian Conacher
106) The Leafs won a seventh game three times (against Boston in the 1959 semi-finals; against Montreal in the 1964 semi-finals; against Detroit in the 1964 finals). The team's seventh game record is 3 wins, 0 losses.
107) The Los Angeles Kings
108) Bob Pulford
109) The Minnesota Fighting Saints
110) Number 5 (Jean Beliveau was given number 4)
111) Bruce Gamble allowed Hull's 50th in 1967, Mike Palmateer let in Secord's 50th in 1983 and Felix Potvin let in Roenick's 50th in 1993.
112) Ballard put blue letters on the Leafs' blue road uniforms, thus making the names indistinguishable.
113) Bobby Baun
114) Andy Bathgate
115) The maple leaf on the front of the team sweater changed to the maple leaf as on the flag of Canada.
116) "Defeat does not rest lightly on their shoulders."
117) Johnny Bower (he played the first period); Terry Sawchuk (second period); and Bruce Gamble (third period)
118) Don Edwards
119) John Brophy
120) Lanny McDonald
121) Bower was the first goalie to receive an assist in the Stanley Cup playoffs.
122) A blue maple leaf
123) St. Michael's College
124) The Leafs defeated the Boston Bruins 3–2.
125) Maurice "Rocket" Richard
126) Ballard was commenting on the removal of the Queen's picture from Maple Leaf Gardens.

127) It was awarded for finishing first in the Canadian division.
128) The Leafs defeated the New York Americans by a 4–1 score.
129) Rogie Vachon
130) Tod Sloan (31 goals) and Sid Smith (30 goals)
131) a) Ace Bailey
b) Charlie Conacher
c) Dave Keon
132) Norm Ullman
133) Terry Sawchuk. Tim Horton, George Armstrong, Red Kelly, Bob Pulford and Allan Stanley helped Sawchuk preserve the lead; Armstrong added a goal into the empty net.
134) Gaetano "Gates" Orlando
135) True (1947; 1948; 1949)
136) The Detroit Red Wings—six times
137) King Clancy
138) Tom Fergus (Illinois); Al Iafrate (Michigan); Jeff Brubaker (Maryland); Rich Costello (Massachusetts)
139) Steve Thomas
140) Wendel Clark, Russ Courtnall and Gary Leeman
141) Wendel Clark
142) Borje Salming
143) Ken Yaremchuk
144) Petr Klima scored on Allan Bester.
145) Dick Duff, John Brophy and Gord Stellick
146) Mike Murphy
147) Tom Watt

John Cullen

Tom Fergus

148) Vincent Damphousse and Russ Courtnall
149) Guy Larose
150) Felix Potvin recorded his first career shutout 4–0.
151) John Cullen
152) Turk Broda and Johnny Bower
153) Mike Johnson
154) Nik Antropov
155) Paul Morris was replaced by Andy Frost.
156) Tomas Kaberle
157) Mats Sundin, who was stopped by John Vanbiesbrouck (Philadelphia) and beat Dominik Hasek (Buffalo)
158) Goalie—Johnny Bower; defence—Tim Horton and Borje Salming; centre—Darryl Sittler; right wing—Lanny McDonald; left wing—Frank Mahovlich
159) Gary Roberts was given number 7, and Shayne Corson was given number 27.
160) Jonas Hoglund was going to be traded to the Boston Bruins for the rights to Kyle Wanvig.
161) The Leafs wore the green and brown uniforms of the Toronto St. Patricks, the team that Conn Smythe purchased in 1927 and turned into the Maple Leafs.
162) Trevor Kidd
163) Tom Fitzgerald
164) The signature of Darryl's late wife, Wendy Sittler, was added to honor her contribution to Darryl's life and career. She passed away from cancer in 2001.
165) Mats Sundin
166) Alex Mogilny (number 89) and Nik Antropov (number 80)
167) Wilf Paiement (99), Sergei Berezin (94), Doug Gilmour (93) and Alexander Godynyuk (93)
168) John Ferguson, Junior.
169) Joe Nieuwendyk.

Wendel Clark

Doug Gilmour

Mike Johnson

Fred Modin

Daniel Marois (#32) moves in on the Minnesota net.

Sylvain Lefebvre (#2) and Jamie Macoun (#34) defend in front of goalie Felix Potvin.

Owen Nolan

Mats Sundin